LEARNING TO WIN

NEGOTIATING - YOUR WAY

by Jenyth Worsley and Natalie Wheen

Contents

The Bargainer's Bill of Rights   **6**

INTRODUCTION   **7**
Negotiating - what it means   *7*
How to use this book   *9*

THE PRINCIPLES OF NEGOTIATION   **13**
What's the scene?   *13*
Basic bargaining   *14*
Know your starting point   *15*
Know your objectives - know your limits   *16*
Plain facts   *16*
Know the other side   *17*
Know your arguments   *18*
Plan your case   *19*
Hidden messages - body language   *20*
The rules of the game   *21*
Your own rules - playing your cards right   *22*
Tricks and deadlocks   *23*
Alternatives   *24*
Half closes   *24*
Closing the deal   *25*
Negotiating skills - key points   *26*

YOU   **27**
Checklist   *28*
Confidence builders   *30*

First impressions 31

Looking the part 32

Using your body 34

The real you 36

Anxieties and fears 38

Anger 39

Needs and interests 40

Your interests 41

Goals and ambitions 42

What are your goals? 43

Lifescenes 44

   1a Buying a car 45

   2a Dispute with neighbours 46

   3a Complaints at a shop 46

   4a Seeing the bank manager 47

   5a Changes at work 48

   6a Dealing with harassment 49

   7a Changes at the office 50

   8a An interview with the boss 51

   9a Union negotiations 52

  10a A public campaign 53

  11a Pitching for new work 54

THEM 55

Checklist 56

Confidence builders 57

Who are they? 58

See them clearly 59

Observing feelings 61

Listening 62

Practise listening 63

Hidden signals 64

Listening for other messages 65

Observation and listening key points 67

Position 68

How things get done 69

Power and interests 70
Lifescenes 71
  1b Buying a car 71
  2b Dealing with neighbours 72
  3b Complaints at a shop 73
  4b Seeing the bank manager 74
  5b Changes at work 75
  6b Dealing with harassment 76
  7b Changes at the office 77
  8b An interview with the boss 78
  9b Union negotiations 79
  10b A public campaign 80
  11b Pitching for new work 81

TECHNIQUES

TECHNIQUES 83
Fact finding 83
Checklist 84
Asking questions 85
Plan your action 87
Getting the message across 89

STRATEGIES

STRATEGIES 93
Preparing a strategy 94
Practising 95
Feeling good - building self-confidence 96
Acting the part 97
Some bargaining ploys 99
Dirty tricks 100
The garden path 102
Lies and deceptions 103
Moving the goal posts 103
Below the belt 104
Always confirm the rule book 107
Before negotiations start 107
Agree a timetable 108
At the end of each meeting 109

Lifescenes   *110*

   1c Buying a car 110
   2c Dispute with neighbours 111
   3c Complaints at a shop 112
   4c Seeing the bank manager 113
   5c Changes at work 114
   6c Dealing with harassment 115
   7c Changes at the office 116
   8c An interview with the boss 117
   9c Union negotiations 118
   10c A public campaign 119
   11c Pitching for new work 121

WORKING TOGETHER   *123*

Who starts?   *125*
Your turn   *126*
Testing   *126*
Carrots   *127*
The Ancient Art   *129*
Half closes   *130*
Problems   *130*
Take your time   *131*
Closing the deal   *133*

FURTHER READING   *135*

The Bargainer's Bill of Rights

- **Your right to respect from other people**
  And that means they shouldn't patronise you, treat you as stupid, or take you for granted. Don't forget that you're as good as anyone.

- **Your right to ask questions**
  They're not going to know what you want unless you ask for it. Don't think your boss is going to give you a rise just because he sees you working hard. He may think that you're slow.

- **Your right to be wrong**
  Stop saying you're sorry, or blaming yourself. We all make mistakes - it's only human.

- **Your right to be unsure**
  Instant decisions may be impulsive and not properly thought out. If you need more time, say so.

- **Your right to say 'no'**
  If you don't think the offer is good enough, then say so.

- **Your right to say nothing**
  This is always a useful tactic. Silence embarrasses people, and often they say things they don't mean to, just to fill the gap. Don't be persuaded.

- **Your right to repeat yourself**
  People don't remember everything they're told first time, so, if it's important, tell them what you want them to hear again. It'll impress them with your belief in your own arguments.

- **Your right to have your own space**
  This means more than physical space - a powerful personality often makes us go with them whatever we ourselves really want to say or do.

Introduction

NEGOTIATING – WHAT IT MEANS

Negotiate is a word we hear a lot about nowadays. It conjures up images of arms talks, takeover bids or wage deals. 'Big' situations where large organisations argue with each other, or workers ask for more money and managements offer too little in return. It all feels a long way away from people like us.

But in fact, we all spend time negotiating in everyday life - and there are a lot of simpler words which let us get closer to the idea. Such as: bargain, deal, discuss, manage, work out. A dictionary will say that to negotiate is something like: 'discuss around the subject with the aim of coming to an agreement'. Negotiation is finding ways to get around a problem, to compromise, to get to the result everyone accepts.

Because most situations are not clear-cut, a win for one side does not have to mean that the other side loses. People can have different aims, different interests. Often the best solution offers each side what they really want and professional negotiators recognise that win-win is better than win-lose.

It's the same with our friends or our families and partners. Most people are as concerned at keeping a good relationship going as they are at getting what they want. Even with strangers, like those we deal with in shops or in the street, we generally get a better response by also considering their point of view, even though we may have to take a strong line with them in the end.

Nothing in democratic society is fixed and unmovable: the more we are prepared to discuss an issue, the more we can shape the outcome.

Start simple

One of the basic bargaining places is a market stall: the seller asks far too much money and you offer far too little. You both talk, discuss, play a few 'games' with each other and eventually come to a figure which you both consider to be fair.

You've actually worked out a price that's right for both buyer and seller.

Think sideways

That final price also means something else which is less obvious. It reflects how important it was for the buyer to purchase and the seller to sell that particular article.

He'd have come down further if he was desperate to get rid of a job lot. While if you weren't seriously interested, you wouldn't have bothered to start the bargaining game. Moreover, if you really wanted it badly, you might even agree a higher price.

At the top end

Of course, negotiation can be a very sophisticated process employing skilled professionals. These people usually work for large groups like governments, unions, or managements. They're very highly trained and negotiating is their job.

Since negotiating is a skill that can be taught, it follows that anyone can start to learn, without necessarily intending to negotiate professionally. Learning what goes into it is going to help in all kinds of everyday situations.

What's involved?

In most situations, we have to deal with someone else to reach agreement, even if it's only working out which film to see with friends.

But to have a proper **discussion** you need to have **information**: what films are on, at what time, at which theatres. There are **techniques** for collecting information and in presenting your case effectively.

Finally, there are ways of planning the action so that your point of view has a better chance of being taken on board. It's called **strategy** and it can be used positively and negatively.

You can look at it all as a game, with rules, techniques and skills to be learnt and practised on your own before you use them in the match.

That's the point of this book: to build up blocks of skills which will all add up together. In the chapters that follow, there'll be two kinds of information: practical techniques on how to work through the process of negotiating - and also personal skills based on self knowledge, because you'll find you need to understand yourself a little to be able to negotiate on your own behalf!

HOW TO USE THIS BOOK

You'll find *Negotiating - your way* contains six parts, apart from the Introduction.

Basic Principles Introducing the various elements you can find in a negotiating situation and what they mean in practice.

You Finding out what kind of a person you are: your strengths, reactions and any negative feelings you might have about yourself; your needs, goals and ambitions.

Them Finding out as much as possible about the other side's position and needs.

Techniques Developing simple skills to help you prepare a strong case and to use in supporting your argument.

Strategies Planning the negotiations to enable you to make your own point and override any negative tactics or diversions from the other side.

Working Together Mutual cooperation to achieve a common goal; working through step by step, until both sides are satisfied.

Each chapter concentrates on a particular block of skills related to that topic, all the skills relate to each other, and the blocks together make up the main foundations of good negotiating. The skills involved are familiar to many of us in everyday life, but because we're all different, each person will find some easier than others.

Start by reading the opening section on Basic Principles, just to find out or remind yourself what is involved. By the end, you'll get an idea of where **you** want to begin.

Subsequent chapters start off with a set of questions - a Checklist - to find out your reactions to different situations. And at the end of three of the chapters there are a number of Lifescenes, illustrating some problems people may encounter in their personal lives, at work and with a group of people.

Some of the Lifescenes may cover a problem that you have had to face. From the Checklists you can work out more specifically your own starting point to learning more. The symbol **SEE ➥ pXX** will act as a guide to the relevant sections. You'll probably find you want to concentrate on some parts of the book more than others.

You can also go back to a section and look at it again from a different viewpoint. You may have worked on your own personal feelings - your hopes, aims, fears and so on. You could try thinking about the situation in question from the other party's point of view. You can think about strategies and techniques from both sides too.

That's just what the book is for - to use according to your own needs, designing your own plan of action. Jump about, skip sections and chapters, find out more as you feel necessary.

Or start at the beginning and work on!

Use the circles to help you think about your next step.
Photocopy the diagram and cut along the dotted line.
Rotate the inner circle to get four different sets of
viewpoints on each set of topics.

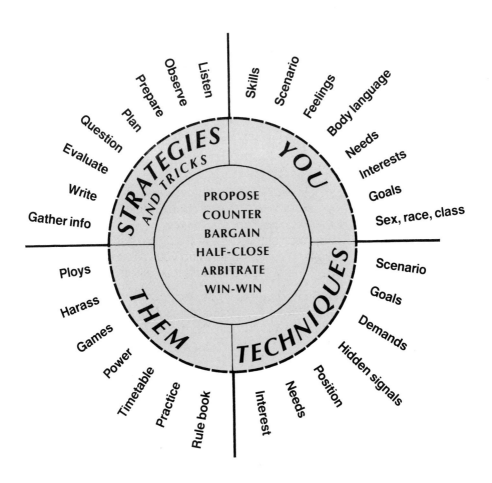

This book is not a book you have to work through from beginning to end. You set the goals you want to achieve. It's up to you to choose what level to work at; only you will know if you're satisfied with what you achieve.

The outer circle reminds you that your primary goal is negotiating to a satisfactory solution.

You and They - the two sides in the process. You have to find out how to work together.

Both sides need to know techniques for negotiating and to plan their strategies. In the centre is the negotiating situation: the two sides meet and start discussions using their skills, techniques and strategies.

But:

Each side also brings a whole **hidden agenda** to the negotiations. The more you know about what could be going on 'behind the scenes', the better you can deal with the effects. You have a stronger hand to play when you're negotiating.

Versatility comes with practice: put yourself in their shoes, think about the information they will have about you, prepare to counteract their strategy, find out before a meeting exactly what their limits are.

Spin the circle and examine your feelings in each kind of situation.

Think about each possible situation.
Think about how you respond to it.
Break down the action into small parts.
Work on those little by little.
Start building the parts back together.

The Principles of Negotiation

Your starting point is usually that you have a goal in your mind which at first seems difficult or even impossible to achieve. You can't see how you can get there, given the obstacles in the way. Whether they're real or imaginary, they stop you thinking clearly.

Successful bargaining comes from breaking up the problem into a simple series of steps. The very first one is to look at the situation clearly. Then you should be able to sort out in your own mind what the difficulties might be **before** you start discussing the matter with the other side.

Put yourself into a neutral middle ground so you can start to look calmly at what is possible and agreeable to both sides.

After that, you can start to work on the information you will need to have with you to make your case as strong as possible.

WHAT'S THE SCENE?

Here are two possible occasions for bargaining. Use them as a starting point to think of appropriate bargaining steps to think of what people might say to each other, what the arguments might be, what kind of conclusions might be reached in the particular circumstances.

One of your friends is selling an office lamp you will find very useful. You notice the switch has gone, which means you would have to spend a little more to get it to work properly. So you offer less than the asking price to compensate for the cost of the repair, although you don't want to haggle with a friend.

Would you decide you wanted the lamp at any price?
How carefully would you look at its condition?
How would you work out your offer?
Could you persuade your friend to reduce the price?

There's a rush order at work and your group wants to get the job out on time. You've all agreed to speed up the productivity in return for good bonuses. But while some of the group want to stay on late to get it done, most people want to work through their lunch hour. You need to get home on time in the evenings, but the break from work mid-day is necessary, given the noise in the workshops. You suggest the group should work out how long the job will take and agree to start work earlier to get it done.

BASIC BARGAINING

Let's start with the basic facts of any bargaining situation.

1   You have a case or a viewpoint or a need and you have to be able to express that clearly so that it can be understood easily.

2   In order to have your case understood, you need to make people listen to your case: you want them to recognise your position.

3   Negotiation becomes easier if you meet the other party half-way. If you can understand their position and their interests, you can put your case in terms they find familiar or reasonable.

4   Think of several ways of getting to your goal. If you can suggest alternative approaches, it's very difficult for anyone to say no to everything all the time.

5   Break up the argument into small sections and try to reach agreement step by step. The more steps you agree along the way, the easier it is to reach final acceptance.

6   Make sure you know as much as you can about the options open to you. Don't go for black or white but look at the grey areas to see where you can give or take a little.

| START SIMPLE |

KNOW YOUR STARTING POINT

Most negotiations start because you want to change the present situation: you want a pay-rise, to sort out an argument, to agree on a plan of action.

However, the **feeling** behind what you really want is going to colour every step you take in sorting out a result. It's important to sort out what kind of emotional interest you have in the situation.

for example   *What are your aims?*

You bought a new shirt and a sleeve fell out in the first wash. You take it back to the shop.

Do you want ...

another shirt in exchange?

your money back so you can buy something else (the shirt was a mistake anyway)?

recognition of the bother it's caused?

You're going to ask your boss for a pay-rise which recognises the extra work you do at the office.

Do you want ...

a straight exchange?

extra money for extra work?

recognition of the good job you're doing?

to get your own back on the others in the office?

to achieve promotion over them with more pay?

What are you really negotiating for? What is your hidden motivation?

emotional satisfaction?

fair play to be done?

to calm down an uncomfortable situation?

to get a solution to a problem?

to satisfy your personal needs and interests?

What else?

KNOW YOUR OBJECTIVES - KNOW YOUR LIMITS

Before you start any negotiation, be absolutely clear in your own mind exactly what you're asking for - your **target**.

This gives you a definite goal to work towards.

However, most negotiations involve some kind of compromise, so you also need to know how far you could move from your target. You need to think about the **least** you'll settle for, any **optional** plans you could agree to and what parts of your shopping list' you could drop if it meant definitely winning a more important point.

You may even need to consider a solution that's offered in kind: extra work space in recognition of your status; luncheon vouchers instead of cash; an extra low-interest bank loan facility.

Decide on your goals.

1   Make a list of your objectives relevant to your situation.
2   Break them up into separate sections.
3   Set out all the parts in order of importance.
4   Make a separate list of possible alternatives to your point of view which you could think about.

Think of the points that are absolutely necessary to you, the parts you could be flexible about, and the parts you would be happy to give way on, in exchange for a firm agreement on a point of greater importance to you.

PLAIN FACTS

The more you know about your case, the more convincing you'll sound to the other side. The more information you have to support your arguments, the more confident you'll feel.

If you really work out what the issues are, you'll be ready with all the answers, able to cope with any point the other side chooses to raise.

Plain facts are very important to sort out the basic issues from the emotional background. If you can keep the facts separate from your feelings, you're not going to be distracted by personalities, attitudes and psychological tricks.

Plain facts clearly set out the real situation, such as:

- The number of times you are woken up at 3 am by your neighbour's motorbike.

- Your official job description in comparison with your actual work load; your qualifications and work experience; your record of good work and your salary in comparison to the local average.

- The number of times a ball has been kicked on to your balcony by the grandchildren of the old couple in the next flat.

- The way a new development will change the present environment: heavy traffic on narrow roads; a new hazard at a school crossing; overloading the public services.

KNOW THE OTHER SIDE

The more you can find out about what the other side is doing, the more you're going to be prepared for the points of view they'll advance to argue their case. This applies whether you're negotiating with your next-door neighbour, or with the personnel department in a big multi-national company; the better picture you can build up of their position, the greater your advantage.

Understanding the other side's real interests or problems could be the key to how you plan your moves.

And it's important to realise that just as you have emotional needs and personal pressures colouring your demands - so does the party you're negotiating with.

Why are they behaving as they are?
Are there unseen pressures?
Is there something they are trying to conceal?

- Your neighbour with the noisy motorbike dresses tough in black leather with studs; he never ever speaks to anyone in the street.
  In fact, he is actually very shy and uses the gear to hide behind. It does the speaking for him.

- Your pay is less than your colleagues.
  In fact, your company is looking for redundancies and the first to go will be the highest paid.

- The old couple in the next flat allow their noisy grandchildren to run riot whenever they and their parents come to visit.
  In fact, the old couple's son and daughter-in-law have to be humoured on their visits, otherwise they'd spend their time arguing and probably not bother to come. The old couple get lonely.

- The town council are giving high priority to outside businesses coming in.
  In fact, your town is in a development area and will attract good grants for new sunrise industries providing jobs with a future.

To understand **their** position, think of what could be going on behind what you can see.

KNOW YOUR ARGUMENTS

Information is a powerful weapon. When you make a statement, make sure that you have the supporting evidence to back it up.

a   Several people in the street have complained to you about the motor bike noise.

b   You know your present pay is too low because two colleagues doing the same work are paid more. You've asked them and you have the figures.

c   The grandchildren of the old couple have taken to visiting without their parents and they are even more out of control then.

d You know the new development will damage the roads because you have figures from previous occasions. You've taken expert advice from the Police Road Safety department and the motoring organisations.

Look for supporting information
When you are researching your facts, you always need to look beyond the obvious. For instance, each of the situations above could raise further questions.

a Do you know what the regulations are regarding vehicle noise levels? And have you made any attempt to talk to the shy bike rider?

b Have you discussed the matter with your trades union representative and have you checked your contract of employment and incremental awards?

c Could the reason for the children's disturbed behaviour be that their parents' marriage is breaking up?

d Are your figures up to date and relevant? Have you sought expert opinion about re-routing traffic?

PLAN YOUR CASE

Once you've worked out a point of view carefully, it's important that you get that point of view across to the other party. It's very easy to get flustered and lose your cool, or to start rambling, losing the point, forgetting half of what you want to say. So work out what you want to say and write it down. Work out some possible responses and practise several responses to an argument, each with their own supporting facts.

You can make people listen by speaking

- clearly
- simply
- coolly
- logically
- to the point

And that comes with planning how to present all your facts in a coherent order.

What you want	*what you are negotiating for*
Why you want it	*your needs and interests*
Arguments for and against it	*the options*
Facts and figures	*to prove your point*

HIDDEN MESSAGES - BODY LANGUAGE

You can get on the road to success by showing that you're confident without saying a word. Even if you believe you've hardly a chance, don't show it! Actors work on how to present a character **before** they get in front of the audience. With a little practice the rest of us can also show our characters in a positive way. In any negotiation, it's very important to give yourself that extra advantage.

Take a deep breath before you start, collect yourself. Like an actor, you're making an entrance, you look interested, you lean forward to participate in the conversation and to command attention.

Take a critical look at the responses you're getting - body language speaks just as loudly from them to you.

What are they doing when **you're** speaking?
What are they doing when **they** talk?

In many formal meetings you'll find people:

- doodling
- shuffling through papers
- looking away from the discussion
- holding their head in their hands
- not looking at you when they talk
- playing with an object as they speak
- carrying on a conversation in asides

You can find out a lot about people's attitudes by observing them, so notice the signals. But don't interpret them too hastily. One person may frown when they disagree with you, another could be considering your words very carefully. So double check out what the signal means if you can.

Keep them interested

In any discussion, it's important the other side keeps up with the points you're making. You need to be prepared to lead the discussion and, in doing so, to make sure:

- they understand what you're saying
- they respond to what you say
- they are properly considering your point of view

You need to break into any possible resistance or lack of concentration to make them sit up, lean forward and take a positive part in the proceedings.

Useful tactics include:

- asking questions along the way
- inviting a response at regular points
- causing silences to make people want to speak out

THE RULES OF THE GAME

In a formal negotiation it is very important to agree the ground rules before you start, or you may find all your hard work slipping away.

The easiest get-out in the world is for a company rep to say he hasn't the authority to take a decision and will have to refer to someone else. Then you have to go through the whole process again.

You can agree all the principles involved for a wage increase - but have everything fall down on the timing.

You're discussing your problem quite successfully and then the other party suddenly adds another problem which is not strictly related to the matter in hand.

To get around these diversions there are conventions in negotiating, which you usually agree before you start on the main issues:

The status of the negotiators - do they have the *authority* to make decisions; if not, how far does their authority to negotiate go?

An agenda - a list of topics to be discussed and agreed. No other points will be allowed in to the discussions subsequently unless both sides agree.

The purpose of the negotiation - is it to reach an informal agreement, or a binding resolution which both sides must keep? If it results in a formal contract, what details should be written into the contract?

Timing and time-scale - how long should the discussions be allowed to go on for? Some powerful organisations can deliberately string them out. How long are the agreements going to be effective, will they be back-dated, when will they need revising?

NOTE You may find that unwritten rules also apply, and one of the most common is for business to be done in the bar or even in the gents or ladies!

YOUR OWN RULES - PLAYING YOUR CARDS RIGHT

This is like looking at a hand of cards; what are your strong suits, your high and low cards, your trumps - and the joker in the pack. Don't give away your winners. Make a big play of giving away your losers....

It's all a question of **strategy.** You know what you want, why you want it. Now comes **how** you're going to get it.

Of course, you have to start with a logical sequence of where you'd like to get to - a list of all the points you need to agree and the conclusions you need to reach.

But you have to see how your arguments are going to work with the other side. Try playing the opposite role and question the validity of your own arguments.

By working out the arguments **against** your own, you should be able to counteract them more effectively.

Then think of your approach: what tone are you going to choose? - pushy, relaxed, self-righteous, angry, appeasing?

Do you want to emphasise or to disguise your main theme?

TRICKS AND DEADLOCKS

There are a number of tactics the other side can employ to put you at a disadvantage. They range from giving you a seat with the light in your eyes - so that you can't see the other party's face clearly - to taking or making distracting telephone calls during the meeting.

In an informal context, you might find your partner insists on having children or pets in the same room.

In many big companies and corporations, delay and postponements are standard practice. They may even argue that the problems you want to discuss have nothing to do with **them.**

There are ways of trying to force their hand, such as walking out of the meeting or making threats of some severe action like striking, non-cooperation, or causing a nuisance.

But beware of falling into their trap.

ALTERNATIVES

When you are working out your strategy, always remember you don't have to settle for everything. You can look for a BATNA, a Best Alternative To A Negotiated Agreement. In other words, what you could live with if you can - get your ideal solution.

It means going back to first principles to consider what your needs and your options really are. For instance, when arguing for a pay rise or better work conditions, you are in a stronger position if you know someone else has been after your talents for some time and offered you a job. Consequently, a threat of dismissal isn't really a threat.

Arbitration

Getting out of what seems to be a dead end is often tricky. If you've reached the point where there's nothing you can say to each other, consider consulting an expert who can judge the best course for both sides impartially.

Arbitration, of the professional kind, goes through all the arguments one by one to find areas where agreement can start. You can also act as your own arbitrator:

- Play 'what if... ' games with the options, looking equally at what each side is saying.

- Draw up circle charts on what you've agreed so far to see how the various bits can link up.

- Brainstorm ideas. Here anything goes and you make sense of it all after the session stops.

HALF CLOSES

At the start of any discussion, it often seems that the goal is miles away, that the other party is never going to agree to your requests, that there's a big inequality in power between the two sides.

It all seems much easier and much more possible if the steps you plan are little steps; that you work your way up to the big 'Yes' by a series of smaller ones.

A little 'yes' doesn't even have to be part of your list of objectives. It's all to do with making sure that the other side is listening.

You want to get the other side to agree:

- that you have a problem or a grievance
- that you want to discuss it
- that it is in both parties' interest to discuss it

A half-close is about making the other side catch the ball, it keeps them in the discussion, it keeps the arguments alive.

Half-closes are well-timed questions inviting agreement, usually, quite simple, which make you feel very foolish if you don t respond to them.

"Am I right in thinking ..."
"I'm sure we would all agree, wouldn't we ..."

CLOSING THE DEAL

Closing the deal can be the hardest part of it all.

Again, it helps to progress slowly:

- go over the main areas of the problem you're discussing, point by point.
- **summarise** what you've discussed so far
- **emphasise** what you've agreed
- **extract** the points still to be agreed

Start off by saying something like:

"Well, I think we've sorted out most of the details - if I could just summarise ..." or

"Could we just stop a minute to recap on where we've got to so far ..."

And then, concentrate the discussion on the final points one by one.

Make sure you make a record of what has been agreed, and make sure it's written down and signed by both sides.

NEGOTIATING SKILLS - KEY POINTS

Summary   Know your aims

What are your feelings?

Know your objectives

Know your limits

What are your goals?

Plain facts

Know the other side

Gather your arguments

Plan your case

Watch out for body language

Know the rules of the game

Work out your own game

Tricks and deadlocks

Arbitrations and alternatives

Half-closes

Closing the deal

You

The first and most important person in any negotiation is you.

Your needs and interests

Your personal concerns at home, at work, with a group

What you are like as a person

Your strong points and your weak ones
Your irritating habits
What turns you on
What makes you lose your temper
Your hopes, anxieties, ambitions

Right from the start, most of us get bogged down in details and problems which have nothing to do with the negotiations at all. We worry about how people look, their status compared to ours, their accents, temper, even the way they dress. These are all kinds of silly but simple diversions – if you look at them clearly, you can see they aren't really problems at all!

So first we need to find out the difference between what we want and what is getting in the way of our goals - and that means finding out what makes us tick.

Most of us hardly ever stop to think for long about ourselves, we're so busy worrying about the rest of the world and what they think of us. But of course, the more we do ask questions of ourselves, the more answers we get: the more we know, the more confident we are.

HOW WELL DO YOU KNOW YOURSELF?

✓ CHECKLIST

YES	NO	SOME-TIMES

Their feelings. Do you ...

Get flustered easily ?

Like making a fuss?

Hate complaining, except at home?

Have a low flash point?

Feel put down by authority?

Making a good case for yourself. Do you ...

Like making an entrance?

Get very nervous speaking in public?

Assert yourself calmly if you are harassed?

Getting on with others. Do you / are you ...

Find it hard to tell what they are thinking?

A good listener?

Read their body language easily?

Able to motivate and control a group?

Find it easy to see their point of view?

YES	NO	SOME-TIMES

Finding out.   Do you …

☐	☐	☐

Know your way around a library?

Have good interview skills?

Know your legal rights on consumer goods?

Know who to ask for advice?

Analysing a situation.   Can you …

Sort out possible courses of action?

Work out what steps to take?

Recognise a dirty trick when you see one?

Going ahead.   Do you / are you …

Enjoy getting a good bargain?

Always make sure of your facts?

Make the best of your appearance?

Have a good command of tactics and strategy?

Unafraid to use a few dirty tricks yourself?

Able to take the long-term view?

CONFIDENCE BUILDERS

When you have filled in the questions on pages 28 and 29, have a look at the pattern of your answers.

If you answered **YES** to most of them, you are fairly confident about yourself. If you answered **NO** or **Sometimes** to most of the questions, it looks as if you don't have much confidence in yourself. Before reading further, go back to page 6 and have another look at the Bargainer's Bill of Rights.

The most important is the **right to respect from other people.** Which sounds fine. But it's hard to respect people if they show by their actions or their feelings that they don't respect themselves. If you don't really respect yourself, can someone else?

And it's a vicious circle. The more people take you for granted, or abuse you or don't listen to your opinions, the lower your own self-esteem drops. And if you are out of work and can't get a job, that makes you feel even lower.

So the rest of this chapter contains pointers to learning more about yourself and building up your confidence, so that you can show your family, your friends and potential employers that you know what your true worth is.

The areas are:
* first impressions
* the real you
* fears and anxieties
* needs and interests
* goals and ambitions
* special skills

Learning about yourself is not something that can happen overnight. Like the negotiating process, it has to be broken up into blocks for you to work on and develop little by little.

FIRST IMPRESSIONS

Whenever we meet someone, we react to all sorts of signals that they give out. What colour clothes are they wearing? Does it suit them? Do they look at us straight in the eye? Do they hold themselves confidently? Do they have a friendly smile and seem pleased to see us? Is their voice pleasant to listen to?

When we communicate with other people, up to 70% of the information we give out is actually non-verbal. With all these factors saying things about us, whether we like it or not, it's better to be in control of that 70%.

Your appearance

If you look good, you feel good. This goes right down to basics like having clean and well-styled hair, clean fingernails, wearing colours that suit you, wearing clothes that are appropriate for the occasion.

If you are going to take a Sunday afternoon boating trip, you could feel out of place in a city suit. At an interview with the bank manager, you would do better to wear the suit instead of more casual clothes.

It's really a tactic in the game of getting what you want. If you live up to the bank manager's expectations in what seems like a small thing such as dress, you can get down right away to negotiating the more important issue of an overdraft. You don't have to fight a hidden battle of prejudice - "Why can't this person respect my status as a bank manager and dress the way I think they should?"

Have a look at yourself objectively. Would you look better with a different hairstyle, brighter colours, ironed shirts? If you saw yourself across a crowded room, would you want to go and talk to that interesting person?

Or are you hidden in the crowd?

LOOKING THE PART

How you look and the clothes you wear give immediate signs as to the sort of people you mix with and know, your standards, your age and attitudes.

If you think someone's attractive you are inclined to like them. Good qualities are also linked together so a good looking man will often be taken for a successful and clever one too. Being attractive isn't just beauty, though. It's to do with how well you look after yourself, the whiteness of your teeth and the smile on your face. Sex appeal comes in as well. However out of place it may seem, people do react to you as a sexual being.

Feeling you look right will also give you a lot more confidence. Fashions and conventions change so fast, but there are some general rules to help:

Adapt Before walking into a new situation, think carefully. Picture what the likely style of dress will be. A solicitor, for example, generally dresses formally in a dark suit whereas the people working on a fashion magazine will be more casual and trendy. To get used to noticing what people wear, you might like to think of someone you met today and pencil in your impressions about them in the table on the next page before you try the exercise out on yourself.

Fitting in with the norms of the group you're with puts you all on the same footing. They can feel comfortable with your appearance and instead of only thinking 'How does she think she can get away with that shade of purple?', they start listening to what you have to say and finding out what you are really like.

Be smart Dressing smartly is generally a sign of authority. Do not confuse this with over-dressing however, as this may have the opposite effect of making you look out of place and stupid.

Colour   Is a good way to express your personality when you feel restricted by style. Current theories claim that we each fit into a seasonal colour scheme which determines those colours that complement and those that detract from our appearance.

Photocopy the table below and fill in your idea of how you look. Now ask a friend who knows how you spend your time to do the same thing for you. Encourage your friend to be honest and say what is really thought. Then compare the two tables and discuss any differences.

SCALE **1-5**

☐	clean	☐	soiled
☐	tidy	☐	scruffy
☐	fashionable	☐	outdated
☐	attractive	☐	off-putting
☐	comfortable looking	☐	awkward-looking
☐	appropriate	☐	unsuitable

What suits you?

Formal or casual: _____

Colours: _____

Pale or bright: _____

Tight fitting or loose: _____

Length: _____

Accessories: _____

USING YOUR BODY

Of course you can't think about every movement you make. But you can start to be aware of how people use their bodies. This will show you things about yourself and help you adapt to your situation. For example, think back to the last time you had a headache? What had you just been doing? Was there anything that made you feel tense or worried? Pinpointing what set it off could warn you in similar situations in future.

Ask a friend to describe an action or gesture that they associate with you: stroking your hair as you talk, perhaps, or licking your lips, and start checking yourself for it.

What sort of situations does it happen in?

Is there some trigger?

How do other people react to it?

How are you feeling at the time?

Why do you think you do it?

Walk tall

Even from a distance the way you hold yourself and how you move show clearly the sort of person you are and how you feel about yourself. A spring in the step suggests liveliness and good cheer. Rounded shoulders bear the weight of the world.

People treat you as you demand. Just as dressing well and looking good make you appear and feel more confident and in control, standing straight and walking smoothly provide you with an air of ease and openness.

You will have found that people treat you more positively and that you also feel better about yourself. Keep it up.

Boundaries

Everyone sets up a space around themselves which would be threatening to break into. The actual distance depends on how well two people know one another; an intimate friend will come close to touching whereas a stranger will keep at least at arm's length.

How close do you like strangers coming to you? Usually if you are leaning towards someone you show interest; lean back and you could demonstrate indifference or hostility. Friendly proximity does not of course imply closing in threateningly.

Touching

Touch is one of the most important of the senses and, in our sophisticated society, the most neglected. Denial of human contact, like solitary confinement, can quickly cause severe depression.

British codes of behaviour still dictate, however, that we only hug or kiss those we know well. The warmth that another person's touch generates can be conveyed formally by a handshake, preferably a firm one.

Your tone of voice

Your voice brings life to what you are saying. When you feel down, ten to one, your voice will sound colourless and dreary, but you can learn some techniques to help. For instance, if your voice is rather high pitched, keep it lower. If you tend to talk in a loud voice (you'll notice because people will tend to back away from you) try talking quietly for a change. Or maybe you often mumble and can't be heard so you need to be speak more clearly. Nasal voices can be irritating - warm deeper voices in men and women give out a feeling of authority.

Your speech

Some people have no problem in chattering away while others think carefully and have to search for the right words. Think of some people you enjoy listening to. What's different about the way they talk? Do they use long or short words? Do they make you see things in a different way?

Make a recording of your voice on cassette, and listen critically to your normal voice.

Practise some different ways of speaking - this means your style, not your accent. And listen to and copy other people's styles. Is there a DJ or radio presenter who makes you want to continue to listen?

Record a conversation with a friend and notice how you come across. Try talking with a smile, then make yourself sound irritated or bored. Can you notice the difference?

THE REAL YOU

What has happened to us in our life, and what is going on in our private thoughts makes us into the people we are. But it doesn't always show on the outside. We are all a mixture of fears, angers, hopes, ambitions, prejudices, doubts.

When we are dealing with other people we need to make sure we are aware what hidden processes could be influencing us when dealing with our family, at work or at the negotiation table.

Outside factors

There are all kinds of factors which make us into the people we are. They include:

- our social background
- where we live - big city, suburbs, rural village
- our sex and age
- pressure from friends, family or work

Many of these make us prejudiced against strangers or people of other races,or those who are younger or older than ourselves. We don't have to be friends with them, but it is important in any kind of negotiation to be able to detach ourselves from their personality and concentrate on the issues concerned.

Your temperament

This is concerned with how we behave, and how we react in day-to-day situations. For instance, are you:

easily provoked

often depressed

find it hard to concentrate on certain tasks

Most of these states of mind are triggered off by certain events or actions. They become automatic – someone says something and you flare up or you look at a page of figures and your brain refuses to work. It takes practice and self discipline to recognise our trigger points and deal with them. Most of them have to do with anxieties and fears.

ANXIETIES AND FEARS

In the space below, write down up to ten things that happen regularly to you make you anxious. They could be anything from driving in busy traffic to being late for an appointment, having a row with your partner or going into a room full of strangers. Write down five that are mainly in your private life, and five that are mainly to do with work.

Next, give each situation a mark between 1 and 5, to show how stressful you find it. The more stressful, the higher the number.

SCALE **1-5**

☐	1 _____
☐	2 _____
☐	3 _____
☐	4 _____
☐	5 _____
☐	6 _____
☐	7 _____
☐	8 _____
☐	9 _____
☐	10 _____
☐	11 _____
☐	12 _____

If your total score is more than 25, your fears may be getting in the way of your everyday life. It would help you to practice some assertiveness skills.

FURTHER PRACTICE ➡ p90

ANGER

Anger is the reverse side of fear. While fear can paralyse us, anger puts us out of control. The trigger points can often be the same. Impatience over a a delay at a checkout can make us anxious about being late, or it can make us furious about being kept waiting and then we barge in and jump the queue.

Anger stops us from listening.

Anger makes us attack other people and behave unreasonably.

Below, write down 10 situations that make you angry, and to which you usually react strongly. Include situations at home and at work, especially ones that are really trivial, but for some reason make you boil. For example, being contradicted, being kept waiting, or someone's personal habits. You may find that some of them are the same situations that make you anxious or upset.

SCALE **1-5**

☐	1 _____	☐	6 _____
☐	2 _____	☐	7 _____
☐	3 _____	☐	8 _____
☐	4 _____	☐	9 _____
☐	5 _____	☐	10 _____

Then, give each situation a number between 1 and 5 to show how angry that situation makes you.

If your total score is more than 25, your anger may be getting in the way of your everyday life and you may need help in dealing with it. A good place to start is learning how to **listen.**

FURTHER PRACTICE ➡ p62

NEEDS AND INTERESTS

All of us have basic needs as human beings. The most important ones are:

- a sense of security
- to be respected as a person
- a sense of belonging and being loved
- control over one's own life
- a comfortable living and working environment
- a sound financial base

In a situation where we are negotiating or bargaining with someone else, those needs are something we take into account, perhaps without question. You and your family may want to go to different places for a summer break - you disagree, say, over a choice between Blackpool and a boating trip on the Norfolk Broads. But you don't want to provoke such a conflict that would lose the security of your good relationship.

So you give in, to keep the relationship going, but this could mean giving up another need, control over your own life. Is there another way? You could be able to negotiate a solution where both parties are satisfied.

Interests

Your needs, which could be some of those mentioned above, are likely to stay much the same. Your interests may well change from day to day and from one situation to another.

For instance, in deciding where to go on holiday, your basic need would be to have a change from daily routine but your interest could be one of several, such as having a good time/getting a good tan/getting fit/getting away from it all with no washing up.

It's very important to understand your true interests before diving into a decision or laying down your terms.

Turn on to page 45 and read through *Scene la*. Tick the things that could be Angela's interests in her choice of car:

☐ reliability

☐ able to hold a large family

☐ smart, to impress her customers

☐ easy to manoeuvre in town

☐ pleasing her father

☐ pleasing her boyfriend

Angela is not a salesperson, she has no need to impress anyone.

She's single and has no children.

She works in the centre of town and has to cope with rush hour traffic.

So it is likely to be in Angela's interest at this time to go for the car she first thought about, ie a reliable, easy-to-drive mini. It could be in her interest to take her father's advice. It may not be in her interest to listen to Gary.

YOUR INTERESTS

Write down below in one sentence, a current difficult situation which you want to resolve.

_____

_____

What are your interests in that situation?

_____

_____

GOALS AND AMBITIONS

Our interests are also concerned in the goals and ambitions we have for ourselves - both short and long-term.

Long-term goals may include:

- a well-run home
- a job
- a good working environment
- a career structure
- a happy marriage and a wide circle of friends
- lots of kids
- being involved in the community
- financial stability

However, to reach your long term goals you need to take a series of steps along the way, which are your short term goals.

The Prime Minister has said in an interview that the reason she got where she did was because of all those little steps she took along the way throughout her career. Then she was in a good position to take the final step – when she was invited to stand as party leader.

Short-term goals could be:

- training for a better job and pay
- organising your home, office and time more efficiently
- getting on well with your neighbours because you spend most of the time at home
- having more fun by getting to know new people

Exercise

WHAT ARE YOUR GOALS?

In the space below, write down two of your long term goals. Then write down four practical steps that you think you will need to take to get there.

Goals 1 _____

_____

2 _____

_____

Steps 1 _____

2 _____

3 _____

4 _____

CHIEF EXECUTIVE'S OFFICE

Step 4 · · · · · ·
Step 3. Further training
Step 2. Get promotion
Step 1. Get training

LIFESCENES

This chapter ends with twelve situations which may need different skills to resolve. They cover:

1 Personal and private life
2 Problems for one indiviudal at work
3 Situations involving groups of people

After each Lifescene, there are a number of questions for you to consider. They have been designed to give you some knowledge of what aspects of negotiations you would like to work on more, and also to find out more about how you yourself tick.

When you think how you would react if you were in some of these situations, remember your feelings will change when it's to do with the family or if you're at work.

Maybe the best leaders and negotiators bring a touch of the impersonal bargainer into their home, and a touch of playschool into the boardroom.

That is also something you could consider.

1a Buying a car

Angela has been saving up for a year to buy a second-hand car. She now has £750 in the building society which she could use as deposit. Her father, John, tells her to read all the motor magazines before making up her mind. Her boy friend, Gary, wants her to buy a Cortina that a mate of his is selling. She quite fancies a mini, if she can find one with fairly low mileage.

ANGELA   Gary. Listen to this! Mini 1000, W reg. one lady driver, low mileage, vgc £1350. phone 24721 before 6 pm. I wonder what colour it is? W reg. That must be... (counts backwards on her fingers) 1981 or is it '82?

GARY   £1350! It's a rip-off. No car could be in very good condition after being driven 9 years by a lady driver! Come on, Angie. You don't want a mini. Paul's Cortina is a bargain. He looks after it like it was his baby.

ANGELA   Oh yes? Then if I know Paul he'd be up in court by now for baby battering. And no more cracks about lady drivers if you don't mind. I passed my test first go, which is more than you did. I'm going round to see it. You can come if you want.

CONTINUED ➔ p71

Think about what you would do in Angela's place.

Where would you go to get advice? Does asking for professional advice make you nervous?

Do you find it hard to sort out conflicting advice from friends and family?

Do you go ahead once you've made up your mind to do something, or are you easily swayed?

If you found a car that you liked, would you be prepared to bargain over the price?

2a Dispute with neighbours

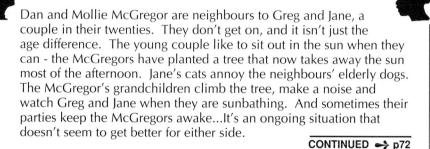

Dan and Mollie McGregor are neighbours to Greg and Jane, a couple in their twenties. They don't get on, and it isn't just the age difference. The young couple like to sit out in the sun when they can - the McGregors have planted a tree that now takes away the sun most of the afternoon. Jane's cats annoy the neighbours' elderly dogs. The McGregor's grandchildren climb the tree, make a noise and watch Greg and Jane when they are sunbathing. And sometimes their parties keep the McGregors awake...It's an ongoing situation that doesn't seem to get better for either side.

CONTINUED ➡ p72

Do you find it difficult to complain when other people annoy you?

Do you explode and have a major row?

Are you able to see their point of view?

Would you be able to suggest ways of improving relations between both sides?

3a Complaints at a shop

Martin has bought a new stereo system from a cut-price discount shop: but ever since he set it up, there has been a distortion of the sound quality when it's played fairly loud. Martin knows a bit about hi-fi and thinks he realises what is wrong. He goes back to the shop and asks for a replacement, but the salesperson doesn't want to know and tries to blind him with technical jargon.

CONTINUED ➡ p73

Are you always sure of your facts?

Do you know what your legal rights are about consumer goods?

Do you get flustered or embarrassed by salespeople who know all the answers?

In this sort of situation, do you usually complain or do you just put up with faulty goods or bad service?

4a Seeing the bank manager

For some years, Jo has been wanting to set up in business running a catering service locally – a service that has already been in demand from friends. At last the decision to go ahead has been taken, and Jo has an appointment with Mr Matthews, the local bank manager, in order to arrange an overdraft as working capital to start off the business. When the appointment was made over the phone, Mr Matthews didn't sound convinced that the scheme would be viable.

CONTINUED ➡ p74

Do you know your bank manager, if only by sight? If not, do you have assumptions about what he's like?

Do you know how to draw up a simple cash flow or business plan?

Are you intimidated by people in professional positions?

Do you think you make the best of yourself when going for a formal interview?

Do you know your bank manager?

5a Changes at work

Eezi-Iyebak Furniture Ltd have had reasonably good staff/ management relations over the years. They have expanded the workforce from 800 to 1500 and have exported their products to Europe. But sales to West Germany dropped last year and competition from Italy has started to make inroads into their market. A new managing director and board of management are determined to improve the design, go for an aggressive marketing strategy and to streamline production. This means streamlining office staff as well as machine operators. So currently, managers have been asked to suggest ways of making their departments more efficient. James Patel, the works supervisor, has been asked by Alec Pringle, production manager, to implement shift and Sunday working with the machine operators, and to bring in part-timers. He believes that the workforce will benefit in the long term from better management, but does not wish to rush into a situation which could result in a confrontation.

CONTINUED ➡ p75

Do you find it easy to express your opinions to people senior to yourself at work?

Do you give yourself enough time to deal with problems concerning other people?

Do you like to see both sides of an argument?

Do you interrupt when people talk to you?

6a Dealing with harassment

Two women, Gina and Lou, are employed as painter/decorators in a firm consisting otherwise of men. They are teased from time to time, and usually keep going with a quick retort, or by ignoring the teasing and putting down the men. But recently, a new manager, Tom, spends much of the time making life very unpleasant for the women. Most of the other workers are embarrassed, but one or two have started to follow Tom's example and no one has told them to shut up. Gina and Lou need strong action to stop Tom's harassment.

CONTINUED ➔ p76

If someone else is being harassed, do you join in or pretend it isn't happening?

If someone treats you as different or puts you down, do you believe that it's really their problem – and perhaps try and work out what they are afraid of?

Is it worse when the harasser is also in authority over you?

If you have been sexually or racially harassed, have you felt able to assert yourself in a non-aggressive manner?

7a Changes at the office

A new laser typesetting system has been installed in the offices of Smartec Designs. Mrs Caplin, the office manager, wants to get the system working soon because it will considerably reduce typesetting costs. The PA to the design director is the only person who happens to have the experience to work it, but he is too busy. Irene and John, the two clerical workers refuse to operate the new equipment because they say it's not their job, although they do have the time.

CONTINUED ➙ p77

Can you think of reasons and incentives to persuade people to undertake work outside their normal field?

What are the main reasons why staff do not want to carry out extra duties?

Have you had to try and implement a scheme which has not been properly thought through? What were the main problems?

Can you think of reasons and incentives to persuade people to undertake work outside their normal field

8a An interview with the boss

Judy Simmonds, a director of a software company, has asked Mark, a new employee who has recently left college, to come and explain his proposals for modifying an accounting package, which are not very clear. Mark is good with figures but not very experienced in dealing with people, and Judy has a reputation for being tough and outspoken.

CONTINUED ➔ p78

What kind of preparation is necessary before meeting a senior manager of a firm?

Would you know where to find the material and how it should be presented?

Can you tell by how a person sits or looks at you if you have their attention?

When you are at a meeting with people, can you tell from little give-away signs what they may be thinking or feeling?

9a Union negotiations

Harry Leadbetter who works for a company which makes marine fitments, has been elected secretary of the branch of his local union. The company has a thriving export trade and sales are up in the UK because of a buoyant leisure market. However, the accelerated growth in electronics has meant that the firm has to move fast to keep up with new production techniques and to research and up-date their products constantly in a new fastmoving market. Anthony Renfrew, son of the founder, wants to bring in young college-trained technicians and phase out the old craftsmen who used to work with his father. Harry, whose father also worked alongside old Sir Anthony, feels loyalty to the firm today, but also to the men and women who have devoted their working life to Renfrew Marine.

CONTINUED ➡ p79

What factors do modern trade union leaders have to take into account when trying to get the best deal for their members?

How do you balance the profitability of the firm (if it goes bust there's no more work) with that of the

employees?

What dirty tricks could an employer use to get his own way? Is there a way of countering them?

What ploys and strategies could the union side use to get a better deal?

10a A public campaign

North Woolford Council is in a difficult position. The traditional industrial base has collapsed! leaving unemployment, urban blight, empty buildings in the old industrial centre and a lower municipal income. The town needs new investment in industry and jobs, new money and a higher national profile.

The Council wants to sell the centre to large property developers who would pull down the old buildings and erect hotels, a leisure and conference centre and transform the environment. Many of the local residents and business people believe this would destroy the traditional north country atmosphere. They would prefer to preserve and restore the centre, bringing in a mix of high-tech industry and small firms, including crafts and community projects. They see it developing as a heritage and leisure centre. Anne Jennings is leading the campaign for the locals.

CONTINUED ➡ p80

What sort of arguments/protests may big business respond to?

How do you arouse the interest of local government, the media etc?

What is the best way of putting forward your case to get maximum publicity?

How long will a campaign of this nature take? Can interest be sustained?

Do you find it hard to keep control when several people are making suggestions at the same time?

11a   Pitching for new work

A large company near Newcastle has recently disbanded some of its specialist departments, deciding to contract out work handled by these departments as necessary. One of them is advertising and promotion. It would be a large job, including handling TV and media, local sponsorship and writing and printing promotional literature. Tyne Teller Associates are a local firm who haven't handled anything so big before, but they are convinced they could make a good job of it. They decide to pitch for the whole contract.

CONTINUED ➔ p81

What sort of decisions would a small company have to make before going for something big?

What information will they need to get before tendering?

How do they go about preparing their case?

How can they guarantee quality and reliability?

What management skills will Tyne directors need to develop?

Them

This chapter is concerned with the other side.

- Whom you are dealing with
- What makes them tick
- How you should approach them
- What you can take for granted about them
- What you need to find out
- How you can tell what they are thinking and feeling
- What their interests and goals are
- What is their bottom line
- The signals they give out

The twelve Lifescenes at the end of the chapter continue the stories started in chapter **You**. They show the other side's point of view. Each raises a set of questions for you to consider. They have been designed to tell you something about your own understanding of other people.

So, are you good at putting yourself in someone else's place? Tick the Checklist and find out.

HOW WELL DO YOU KNOW THE OTHER SIDE?

✅ CHECKLIST

YES	NO	SOME-TIMES

Their feelings. Do you ...

☐ ☐ ☐ Take their emotions into account?

☐ ☐ ☐ Know how different feelings are signposted:

☐ ☐ ☐ Ever put yourself in their shoes?

☐ ☐ ☐ Want them to feel satisfied in a negotiation?

Their manner and appearance. Do you ...

☐ ☐ ☐ Notice how they look?

☐ ☐ ☐ Jump to conclusions about their character?

☐ ☐ ☐ Concentrate on the issues involved, not the personalities?

How they express themselves. Do you ...

☐ ☐ ☐ Notice if they use gestures a lot?

☐ ☐ ☐ Notice if they speak in a differnt way from you?

Their interests. Can you ...

☐ ☐ ☐ Tell how they may react in a given situation?

☐ ☐ ☐ Understand what they need to get out of a negotiation?

☐ ☐ ☐ Understand their problems?

☐ ☐ ☐ Think of ways to satisfy their interests as well as yours?

☐ ☐ ☐ Listen when they put their case?

YES	NO	SOME-TIMES

Their tricks. Can you …

☐ ☐ ☐ Deal with someone who threatens you?

☐ ☐ ☐ Avoid being put down?

☐ ☐ ☐ Keep to a timetable to avoid delays?

The future. Do you …

☐ ☐ ☐ See the value in on-going relationships?

CONFIDENCE BUILDERS

If you answered YES to most of the questions, you have a good awareness of other people.

If you answered **SOMETIMES** or **NO** to most of the questions, you would be advised to read the whole chapter. Any negotiation is a two way process! and it's essential to spend as much time on "them" as it is on yourself.

This includes finding out about:

- their position and power base
- how they communicate
- their interests
- what their values are
- what their personalities are like
- how they react to you
- why they react as they do

When you are able to go into a room or enter into a discussion and know that you understand what the other side is about, it's a lot less frightening for you. And it works both ways. If they see a person who is confident and has obviously thought about their side of an argument, it gives them confidence in you. It can cut out a lot of hassle.

WHO ARE THEY?

Who are these intimidating people you would like to reach an agreement with? They come in all sorts of shapes and sizes and colours and sexes – just like the rest of us. There are a good cross-section of them in the Stories at the end of each chapter. What they all have in common is that they each have a point of view, and it isn't necessarily the same as yours.

Your very first task is to check whether the person you are doing business with is actually the right person. You are returning faulty goods. Does the salesperson have the authority to deal with you, or should you ask to see the manager?

SEE ➡ p73

You want an overdraft facility from the bank. You may find yourself talking to a sub-manager who has to refer to someone else. It will save your time to go direct to that person but the bank, like many large organisations, may prefer to keep you at a distance from the person with power. This takes up more of your time, and more of your patience. If you are short of both, insist on seeing the proper person.

SEE ➡ p74

Other people have their own priorities, deadlines, work quotas, and they won't be the same as yours. Even in your family, indeed sometimes especially in your family, they talk from a position that doesn't really suit you at all.

SEE ➡ p45

SEE THEM CLEARLY

Basically, a negotiation is about two or more people getting together to do something they couldn't achieve by themselves. You can't build a house without buying the bricks. And to do this you must first feel that you know who you're dealing with, so that you trust them and work together.

This section deals with the elements that contribute to developing a working relationship with someone.

As it all concerns you and others, you will find it easier to practise each skill separately in everyday life.

Within minutes of meeting a stranger, you will have formed an impression of what sort of person they are: where they come from, what they do, and what they think of you. And of course they will be doing the same. The picture you both form now could be the one you carry round and refer to automatically whenever you meet. So it's very important to get that picture right.

Exercise

In this photograph, two people have just met. Look at it for about thirty seconds and then answer the questions below.

Whose office is it?

Do they already know each other?

Is one of them going to take the lead?

Now cover the picture with your hand or some paper and try and describe what you saw. Don't add your own interpretation, just be as factual as you can.

Can you remember how they looked?

What were they wearing, the style and condition of their clothes?

What was the expression on their faces?

Their build or figure?

The way they were standing?

Any movement of head or hands?

These are the sorts of things we usually notice about other people straight away, and they can give us valuable clues about their feelings and attitude.

PRACTICE OBSERVATION

If you found it hard to remember what you saw in the photo above, you may need to practise your observation skills, and it's usually easier to do this with a partner.

 A simple test is for two people, 'A' and 'B', to stand and observe each other for one minute. The 'B's turn away while the 'A's change around six items of their appearance - like undoing a button or parting the hair on the other side. 'B' then turns back and has to see what the changes are. Swap over sides.

Some people find this quite difficult. If you are one of those, practise your observation skills in your daily life. Stop every so often, look at something or someone carefully and repeat to yourself what you have just observed. Remember you are after facts, not opinions. Just repeat what you see, not what you think about it!

OBSERVING FEELINGS

We say a lot about ourselves without knowing it, and a good observer can recognise the signals we give out - again, with a little practice.

Here are a few pointers as to how people express themselves:

eye position *looking at the person or looking away*

posture *standing upright or slouched, head to one side or erect, arms folded or moving about*

face *a smile, a frown or a fixed grin*

facial colour *blushing, going pale, white at the corners of the mouth*

breathing *calm, deep breaths or fast, irregular ones*

LISTENING

Listening is a sophisticated activity:

- you hear the sounds a person makes speaking
- you work out the tone of voice they're using
- you understand the content and the meaning
- you listen out for any hidden meanings
- you work out an answer

No wonder it's an important communication tool!

And apart from the information you get by listening, being a good listener helps the other side to relax and have confidence in you.

It's easy to show that you are listening by:

- asking questions
- having good eye contact
- using appropriate body language (by leaning towards the other person or refraining from fidgeting)
- repeating the points made, to show that you've understood them
- keeping an interested note in your voice

Listening well also means hearing what the other party really says, not what we think they said or rather wish they had said!

It's a good idea to recap on what has been said from time to time.

If you can show you're a good listener, the other side will be more inclined to listen to you.

PRACTISE LISTENING

You can easily practise listening techniques by yourself in most everyday situations.

- When someone gives you some information, try to repeat it back to yourself as accurately as you can and in the same way that it was given to you. You could also try this out with a friend.

- Look people straight in the eye when they are talking to you and check if what they say stays in your mind longer.

- Try to recall every story you hear in a single TV or radio news bulletin. If you concentrate on listening you could soon find yourself remembering all the speakers as well as the news items.

But though you can practise listening by yourself as an observer, it's easier with someone else. If you can, try out some of the exercises with a partner, or better still with a group of friends.

with two people

'A' has to tell 'B' something interesting that has happened to them. They speak for about two minutes. 'B' has to repeat what 'A' has said, without any additions and keeping as far as possible to the original order of events. Afterwards, 'A' should tell 'B' if he or she said anything different. Then swap over.

with a group - Chinese Whispers

The group should sit in a circle. One person whispers a short message to the person on the right, who passes it on to their right, continuing until it gets back to the first person.

Make the message a bit longer and ask each person to say it out loud and with the same meaning as the original. Notice how quickly people start using their own words and interpretations.

HIDDEN SIGNALS

Being aware of the hidden signals everyone gives out is a most important tool in negotiating. It is absolutely vital in being able to judge the mood and the success of the discussions.

A really effective negotiator has a fine tuning on how they judge mood, character and atmosphere.

And that's very useful whatever you're doing.

Listening to what isn't being said

You can also **hear** hidden signals from the way people speak. You can actually say one thing with the words and give it quite a different meaning by the way you say it. It's quite easy to get the feel of it – try it yourself with a simple sentence like

'I'm very pleased we're going to see Liz and Jeff.'

Try it:

- pleased
- sarcastic
- angry
- insincere
- shouted
- whispered - and any other way you can think of

Try listening to how people talk to each other in real life - in the same way as you observe people behaving. You can learn a lot from:

- tone of voice
- volume
- projection
  (some people swallow their words, others almost spit them out)
- clarity
- hesitancy
- breath control

Again - it's dangerous to make quick judgments from first impressions, for instance a loud voice doesn't necessarily mean a bossy character: the speaker may have had voice training as an actor, or may be slightly deaf.

Accents may tell you where people have come from, they don't tell you about character or personality.

An abstracted tone of voice might mean that the speaker is actually thinking ahead to possible developments in the conversation.

LISTENING FOR OTHER MESSAGES

Often, the way people talk puts us off hearing what they're saying – so it's important to get over that kind of block. Usually we react instantly to the sound of a voice and we don't go any further.

Finding the true person and listening to the message behind the voice comes with practice.

Listening for **how** people express themselves also helps you to understand more about how they think and how to get information through to them in the best way.

Some people think in pictures _ and use visual descriptions like see, look, focus, clear. Others work with sounds; their words are to do with hearing. The third group will describe with feelings:

- this may **appear** a strange idea
- this **sounds** a strange idea
- this **feels** like a strange idea

Recent research has shown that really good communication happens when two people speak the same 'language' - that means, for example, that they both might use visual descriptions. When there is a communication block, it often happens that the two sides are using completely opposing sets of images.

On the other hand, it is possible to learn a different language – experienced negotiators make a point of matching words and images to those of the person they're talking to.

The next time a friend tells you a story listen carefully to the way in which they describe what happened. What kind of language do they speak?

Do the same the next time you have a disagreement with someone.

Listen also to the way you yourself use language

Does your style match your friend's?
Could you change it to match your friend's?
What about your style in the argument?
Were you using different imagery?

Look at the dialogue on page 77. Has Mrs Caplin listened to what Irene and John were saying?

YES	NO

What sort of language was Irene using?

Visual

Sound

Touch/feeling

What sort of language was John using?

Visual

Sound

Touch/feeling

Did Mrs Caplin respond in the same 'language', or did she use a different one?

Same

With a partner

'A' relates a short story for about one minute. 'B' writes down the key words. Then they swap over. At the end, tell the other person which 'language' or type of words you both use most often.Were you together or opposed?

This will give you a good idea of the way you express yourself most frequently, and it may surprise you. An artist or photographer may use their eyes professionally, but still communicate through one of the other senses, not the visual.

With the same partner, 'A' now tells a story using their most frequently used 'language', while 'B' tries to respond in a different one. For example, 'A' describes what it felt like to go to a new club while 'B' asks if they liked the sound of the music or the look of the clothes people were wearing.

OBSERVATION AND LISTENING - KEY POINTS

Summary
- tone of voice
- facial expression
- physical gestures
- posture
- eye contact

- type of 'language'
- pace of 'language'
- manner of presentation
- physical twitches

- Are you getting clear messages?
- Are words and voice in contradiction?
- What are the gestures adding?

- What does this say about the next step?
- How do I use this knowledge?

POSITION

What the other side is thinking or feeling is only part of the story. You also have to consider their position in relation to yourself, which could include their needs and interests and their power base.

If you look through some of the scenes at the end, you may notice a number of different interests in the other side. They include deadlines, keeping head office happy, keeping the rates down, reducing costs, not provoking a confrontation.

Look through the scenes now, and write down below some of the interests you can pick out.

scene	*interest*

It's worth knowing that someone's **interest** is not necessarily what they **want**, or say that they want. In *Lifescene 5a*, it is in the company's interest to make production more efficient, but it is also very much in the interest of the new management to bring the workforce along with them. The workforce in turn may want things to stay as they are, but it's in their long-term interest to raise productivity or they will simply be out of a job.

In an argument over where to go out for the day, you and your partner may both want to go somewhere different, but it could be in the interest of your long-term relationship to settle on a compromise.

But if one side always gives in, there could be a problem because sooner or later resentment comes to the surface and a good relationship may be damaged. So even if the other side agrees to a course of action, keep looking for the signals to show that they are happy with the arrangement. If they aren't, there could be trouble ahead.

One of the skills in negotiation is to work out beforehand just where both sides' true interests lie, and then to convince them of the case.

SEE ➥ p87

HOW THINGS GET DONE

One of the most frustrating things about dealing with a large organisation is the way they do things - and that often means slowly, and with a lot of bureaucracy.

Every company lays down its own company procedures and rules, and most of them are different. So in business, you have to learn how your other side does business. Once you know, you can begin to use it to your own advantage. For instance:

- Do they make decisions in a team or is one person the key?
- How often are committee meetings held?
- Do the papers go up to head office for approval?
- Does the other side tend to give business to people they meet regularly in the club or pub, or do they seem to prefer a very formal approach?

If you are in business yourself, make a few notes below on how some of the firms you deal with operate.

_____

_____

_____

How could you find out more about their methods?

POWER AND INTERESTS

Often in a negotiation, one side seems to be more powerful than the other. They have the money, the staff. They are the buyers.

On the other hand, you, as an individual or a smaller concern, may have the energy, the ideas and the determination. One of the strongest power bases comes with knowing all the facts and figures before you start - and this includes knowing who you are dealing with in terms of personalities and authority and knowing how to get things moving.

So, research into the other side's **interests**, especially if they are a large concern, is vital for you. This should take into account their current position, the short term future and the long term prospects.

You should be realistic in checking out what will best further their interests, and then in working out if what you have to offer can match those interests. If it won't, then also be realistic and don't waste your time.

Summary   Are you dealing with the right person?
Don't make judgements from first impressions
Practise being able to recognise feelings
Learn the art of listening
Look/listen to/feel other people's 'languages'

Don't be intimidated by the power of an organisation larger than your own

The more you find out about the other side to check that what you offer them is what they really want, the stronger your hand will be.

1b   Buying a car

The mini belongs to Jenni, a social worker who has had a string of troubles with the car recently. She wants to sell quickly and is prepared to come down to £1,200. Although the mileage is low, she drives a lot in town, usually short journeys in heavy traffic. Jenni's an impatient young woman, and hates being left behind at traffic lights, so the engine comes in for a bit of a blasting. 'One driver' is also not quite true. Jenni was given the car by her sister.

JENNI   (on telephone) Social Services department. Yes, that's right, this is 24721. Yes, the mini is still on the market, though mind you I've had three people this lunch time and one couple are coming back at 5.30. Shall we say 4.30? It's a very pretty blue shade. The bodywork is in marvellous condition! But I just have to get a bigger car for my work, you know. I like to take some of my older clients out for a drive now and then.

Shall I be glad to see the back of that car. I've had nothing but trouble for the last six months. Well of course it was lucky I had that bump in April the respray covered a multitude of dents! Nuisance about that couple earlier. I was sure they wanted it.

CONTINUED ➡ p110

Jenni works in social services. That should mean she has a professional and responsible attitude. But can you take it for granted that a professional will be trustworthy in their private life?

She says she needs to sell to get a bigger car. What reasons could a seller have for wanting to sell a second-hand item, apart from wanting to trade up?

2b Dealing with neighbours

MOLLIE *(calling from her bedroom)* Dan, can't you get them to turn the radio down next door? I just can't hear myself think, and you know how bad it is for my nerves.

DAN It's no good, Mollie. Every time I ask Jane she says sorry, and it's down for a few minutes, and then Greg turns up the volume and the whole neighbourhood has to listen to that dreadful racket again.

MOLLIE How they have the nerve to complain about little William and Hamish, I don't know. And it's disgusting, the way they carry on in the garden! I daresay they go round in next to nothing in Majorca, but that's not how I was brought up in Morningside. I'm going over there to give them a piece of my mind.

DAN I think it would be best if I had a chat with Greg first. Maybe Jane hasn't told him how loud the music is through the walls.

CONTINUED ➤ p111

Do you find it easy to understand the point of view of someone who is of a different age or cultural background from yourself?

If Mollie made a practical gesture like babysitting for Jane and Greg, would it affect relations between the two couples?

Do you find that a good row clears the air or makes for more problems when you don't know the other side well?

3b Complaints at a shop

TED Mr Jones, I'm afraid we've had another complaint about the Hi-listen system - the customer bought it last March.

MR JONES He filled in the guarantee didn't he? Then tell him it's nothing to do with us. He'll have to get in touch with the manufacturer direct.

TED But surely...

MR JONES Must I remind you, Ted, we're a fast turnover, low-priced discount store. We don't provide a personal service. He wants personal service, he goes to Harrods. Is that clear?

CONTINUED ➙ p112

When you make a complaint, you have to be sure you are talking to the correct person. Do you know how to find out who that is?

In buying from a discount store, you may be trading price for service. Do you always ask what the terms and service arrangements are before you buy?

Can you think of a way of persuading Mr. Jones to replace your faulty goods now?

4b Seeing the bank manager

MR MATTHEWS Ah, come in, come in. Delighted to see one of our regular customers at last. Now, what can we do for you today?

JO Well if you remember, I wanted to talk about an overdraft for my new catering business. You should have received my outline business plan. I've brought with me a cash flow forecast for the next year, and I think we need something in the order of £5,000.

MR MATTHEWS I'm not sure we shouldn't be talking more in terms of a loan. Say with a moratorium for six months and then repayments in monthly instalments over two years?

JO I would prefer the overdraft. I have a mortgage on my flat, but I'm prepared to use that as security and the interest would be lower than a loan. I see that the bank over the road is offering 2.25% above base rate.

MR MATTHEWS Leave it to me. I'll talk to our loans manager and get back to you after a few days.

JO I would prefer to deal direct with the small business manager if you don't mind. What is his name?

MR MATTHEWS Actually, it's Mrs Roberts. Very well, I'll arrange an appointment with her. Any day next week?

CONTINUED ➔ p113

Banks today have managers for different facilities. It's better to deal direct with the person who can make the decisions.

Did you know that you can bargain for terms with your manager?

Some people don't like to feel they are overdrawn and opt for loans, (which is of course also a debt). Do you have any psychological worries about asking for an overdraft?

5b Changes at work

JAMES I've had a word with our night-shift people, Alec. I've explained the situation and asked if they can suggest ways of stepping up productivity and using our product,on time more efficiently.

ALEC It's quite obvious what needs to be done. Quicker turn around in the workshops and part-timers at week-ends. It's what the board agreed.

JAMES It isn't quite as simple as that. From what I've heard, some of the night shift people would welcome some of the week-end work, and we should be in a better position to speed up the tooling if the operators can work out for themselves where the hold-ups are. You know, we have a loyal workforce and we are one of the largest employers round here. I believe that if we take them with us, it will be better for the company - and will certainly get rid of some of the hassle for us supervisors. Then we can actually concentrate on quality, not on getting the lads moving.

ALEC Yes, you may have a point. I'll put it to the next meeting. Thanks for coming along, James.

CONTINUED ➜ p114

What would be the interests of the tool operators in speeding up production?

What are the interests of the company in consulting the operators?

6b Dealing with harassment

GINA It's getting out of hand, Lou. If that worm puts his oily face near me again I shall strangle him, personally. I mean it.

LOU Yeah, I believe you. Well, as I see it, we've got two options. One, we can think of a way to show him up, make him lose face in front of all his mates.

GINA Or?

LOU Or two, we can get in the union and make an official complaint. He could get the sack.

GINA And good riddance.

LOU OK but I know his family - his kids go to school with mine and Doreen's a good sort. I think we should try it the easier way first - deflate that male ego of his. What do you say, Gina, are you on?

GINA I dunno. It's really getting me down. I'll think about it - but if we do, it will have to be good.

LOU Don't worry, it will.

CONTINUED ➔ p115

Would you agree that most harassment is a power game?

Are there any other ways you can think of to stop harassment?

Can you think of reasons why men resist women coming into their male preserve?

Are there things which women do to give men the wrong ideas?

7b Changes at the office

MRS CAPLIN I've called you in, Irene and John, to see if we can sort out this typesetting business. You know why it's been installed. So tell me what's the problem? Are you telling me you can't do it? You're both good keyboard operators.

JOHN *(Taking a deep breath)* Well I think you should have consulted us before pushing ahead and installing it.

IRENE Yes. You just seem to think that you can pile on the work and we'll get stuck in and do it. If you want the truth, I feel pushed around in this office.

MRS CAPLIN I see.

IRENE All right, I know that new technology is supposed to solve all our problems, but my job has been to type, copy and check it, not do the typesetters' job for them. It's a lot of responsibility.

JOHN Yes and I've done some sums and I've got a good grasp of what the company will save by doing the typesetting in-house.

MRS CAPLIN Let me see if I've got it clear. It's partly the responsibility and partly the money. Is that it?

IRENE And the taking for granted.

CONTINUED ➔ p116

Do the two clerks have their own power base from which to challenge Mrs Caplin?

What are the steps Mrs Caplin could take to improve the situation? She has no authority to increase the clerks' wages by herself.

Do you feel there is good communication between the two sides?

8b   An interview with the boss

MARK   Oh that's just what I need - a summons from La Judy.

GUY   You frightened of her, mate?

MARK   Of course not. But I don't see why I have to go and explain my plan to her - she can read?

GUY   Sure she can read. But she actually likes to hear her new high fliers express themselves in person. So you'd better make sure your facts and figures are together. I assume you have your back-up notes?

MARK   Yes, somewhere. On file.

GUY   Well, I suggest you print them out in your lunch break - not now - and check out your arguments carefully. And any little points she could come at you with. And I should smarten yourself up. This is a high tech business, not a students union meeting.

MARK   OK, point taken. Anything else?

GUY   Since you ask, yes. Judy is having to look after ten programmes a week like yours. She hasn't got time to extract it from you point by point. You've got a good brain - or you wouldn't be here. But in our business there isn't time to write an essay around each paragraph. It's got to be on line first time. Your time and her time costs money - and hers costs more than yours. Right?

CONTINUED ➔ p117

What are the main advantages of preparing your case before an interview?

Are good appearances really necessary? Does it make for rapport?

If your boss is outspoken and demanding, what is the best way of responding?

9b Union negotiations

HARRY Right. I've called this meeting today to discuss the current situation. I take it you've all read the letter from young Anthony?

ALI Yes, it seems clear enough. He wants to throw us out to make room for these so-called modern production methods. Am I right?

PAT It makes my blood boil. Do you remember in 68 - the dock strike? It was us who kept the firm going. As far as I'm concerned, it's out. As from now.

HARRY Pat, you've picked up my very point. If we come out now we'll just play straight into Anthony's hands. I sincerely believe Renfrew's can't carry on without us. But if we move now, we're digging our own grave.

PAT When I think of how his Dad......

HARRY Pat, cool it a moment. Let's just look at it from the firm's point of view. What does Anthony want? Basically he wants quick profits and forget about quality. And he'll bring in new labour to get that - for a time. But I believe that any firm like ours also needs a stable workforce and the youngsters today are always looking over their shoulder to the next job. So I propose we draw up a package which would give us some retraining in the new techniques, and put the case that old-fashioned craftsmanship still has value. What do you say?

CONTINUED ➔ p118

Do you think the interests of the firm and those of the men can be brought together?

Was Harry right in opting for negotiation before strike action?

Do the union put too high a value on loyalty and good workmanship?

10b   A public campaign

ANNE   May I just call the meeting to order for a moment please. Before we go any further I'd like to recap on the position.

The Council as we know, desperately needs to develop our area to bring in new business, improve the amenities and increase employment. I take it that none of us are in disagreement over that.

VOICE   But they are going about it the wrong way. We don't want yet another hotel complex. It will destroy the character of the town, and that's why people come here.

ANNE   Exactly. Now although we object to the Council's scheme, I don't think we have offered a viable alternative. We have to study all the Council's objectives very carefully, and see if we can meet them half way by putting forward our own scheme. Our aims are to use and exploit what this area already has, rather than throwing it away and starting from scratch. So we have to get the public on our side. That means a publicity campaign, including lobbying Councillors and local business people. It also means a realistic assessment of the costs to restore and develop the site; how much investment could be brought in and when returns are likely to come in.

VOICE   But that's not our job.

ANNE   Maybe not, but the bottom line is that the Council will only respond to concrete alternatives - not to opinions and a lot of hot air. So at this meeting, I propose we set up a publicity and media committee, and a planning and finance committee. The next Council meeting on the project is on the fifteenth of next month, so I'd like first proposals by the 6th. Any volunteers, please?

CONTINUED ➜ p119

Is Anne's assessment of the situation a realistic one?

What solutions could the media committee suggest?

What might the planning and finance committee have to take into account?

11b   Pitching for new work

SAHIR   Thanks for coming at such short notice. I saw in today's financial pages an announcement that JBM Holdings is divesting itself of some of its specialist sections and wants to bring in outsiders. One of these is PR and another is systems management.

MANDY   PR? That just has to be for us. Let's go and see them. I know someone in corporate affairs.

SAHIR   Wait a minute, Mandy. We have to think this through very carefully. I agree it could be an opportunity but we don't want to blow it by not doing our homework. So here's what I suggest. Mandy, you talk to your friend, informally, and see if you can find out the company's current policy, and if you can, any future developments. Brian, I want you to look at our own staffing levels. See if there s any spare capacity and how many new staff we would need to buy in to service a JBM account on the systems side, assuming two full-time days a week. Jamilla, what else?

JAMILLA   I think that you and I should look at our current accounts to see who has done business with JBM. Then we need to talk to them to find out what dealings they've had with the firm, and if they have a good reputation in doing business - paying their bills, no dirty tricks, and so on.

SAHIR   Excellent. I'm not going to put us on the line just for the sake of a large contract until I make sure we want to do work with them. And all of us, read the papers and talk to anyone you know who's had connections with JBM. Are there any other points?

CONTINUED ➔ p121

What else should a small firm consider when trying to do business with a large one?

What could be the main pitfalls?

Techniques

The more we practise the basic skills involved in any activity - the better we play it for real. Practice also gives a feeling of confidence. You have a foundation or a home base when you know that you can do it - because you've done it before.

Also, just as in any game, the techniques and skills can be split up and worked at bit by bit. In negotiating, there are simple steps to help you get your act together.

This chapter outlines basic techniques common to most negotiating situations:

- fact finding
- asking questions
- planning the action
- getting the message across

FACT FINDING

Many negotiations break down because one side is not properly prepared. They have not researched into all the relevant facts - on their own side and that of the other. So, if the outcome is important to you, try and gather as much information as possible to make your case watertight.

Start by thinking over what you know about the situation already and decide what more you need to find out.

Brainstorming

This is a valuable way of tapping ideas and is now widely used in industry. It's possible to brainstorm on your own, or with a friend. You will need a large sheet of paper to write down as many ideas as you can - they could be straight facts, further questions, worries. Anything that will help you sort out the real information.

What kind of information do you need? Are you sorting out a dispute over office procedure, or perhaps campaigning against a new development in your town? Or are you locked into silly family arguments?

The information you want will be very different for each of those situations and it's important to get the starting point right so you don't waste time and energy.

CHECKLIST

- *What do you know about the situation already?*
- *What information do you need to find out?*
- *What is the main issue?*
- *Who is directly involved in the discussions?*
- *Is there anyone else concerned?*
- *What are the arguments?*
- *Are there hidden issues like money problems, family arguments, ill-health ?*
- *What facts do you know for certain?*
- *What facts do you need to check?*

Further research What kind of information is necessary:

known facts, like a job description or a Law?

expert opinions?

background knowledge?

Where are the best places to find out:

- libraries?
- local newspaper?
- company reports?
- specialist publications e.g. trade magazines?
- Citizen's Advice Bureau, solicitor, doctor?
- local Council, Government department, Unions?

On personal matters, it may be a question of observing and listening, taking the trouble to work out why a person does something. They may be bad-tempered because they're ill - or tired after a lot of chores at home. You can find out a great deal by just observing.

Put the info together

Collecting facts is only useful if you can put those facts to work for you. That means you need to make some sense of what you've learnt, analyse your results, and work out a plan of campaign.

ASKING QUESTIONS

There isn't a more direct way of finding out - whether you want information for yourself before you go into a negotiation, or whether you want it straight from the other side during your meeting.

However, you can be clever about how you ask a question. There are various ways of going about it and they usually get quite different answers:

'How is Mum feeling today?' - *'Better than yesterday.'*

'Is your Mum better?' - *'No'*

Some questions invite specific answers:

'How old are you?' - *'Twenty-three'*

With some of them you can't get away from the implied consequences:

'Do you agree that punctuality is important?

Sometimes you're given an open door to say what you like:

'What do you think will happen with the new shopping mall in the middle of town?'

Sometimes there's no answer expected:

'Do you really expect me to believe that?'

The question game

It can be interesting to try out various ways of asking questions to see how the answers can change. Try it with a simple question which can be asked in several ways.

When you feel comfortable doing that, try asking one person the same question over and over again - but each time you ask it, disguise the way you put the question, and approach from a different angle. You'll find that the different ways the question is answered give out a lot of information.

You notice also that if you start questions with the words: 'Why....' or, 'But don't you think that.....' the answers usually sound defensive. They are threatening ways of talking to people and they don't bring out very much information. Check that out with what you can often hear on news programmes on radio and TV.

Ask questions to clarify

In negotiating, it's also essential to ask a question if you feel you don't understand something or you want some more information on it. It often happens that the other side then realises that their arguments don't make sense or appear unreasonable.

Sometimes you might want to ask difficult questions in advance so that the other side can prepare a proper and accurate answer to your points.

Some useful phrases

'Am I right in thinking....?'
'Could you please explain......?'
'How do you feel....?'
'What do you mean by....?'
'What is your authority for this statement....?'

PLAN YOUR ACTION

Your **starting point** is your knowledge of what you want.

Your **end point** is getting what you want - or as close as you can to your goal.

A good route plan helps you to use your resources well along the way.

Sort out priorities

You could think of the issues as a hand of cards: the low value cards go into play to keep the game going until you have a chance to win with a high card. Jacks, Queens and Kings are your main points and you don't want to waste them. Your Trumps have the kind of information the other side can't argue with. And the Joker - well that's up to you...

You also know quite a lot about what the other side has to play with, from all the background information you've gathered to support your case. You can actually have practice runs on how your negotiating might go by playing that useful game 'What if' with your various points.

Make a list of every detail that you want agreed and then list those details in order of importance.

Make sure that you clearly know:

- those matters you want agreed absolutely
- those you could accept a slight variation on

- those you could be very flexible about - or even give up if it helped a gain elsewhere

You also need to know why something is important so try to support your listing with added information that you feel clear about.

Ask yourself:
- exactly what do I want?
- why do I want it?
- how important is it to me?
- how much satisfaction will I get from it?

for example At work, your boss has been giving you much more to do than the other secretaries, but he hasn't shown any recognition of the extra responsibility he's put on to you.

Your list of wants could read:

a rise in salary	*because of the extra work*
word-processor	*for the extra work-load*
re-grading	*in recognition of responsibility*
acoustic screening	*less distractions*
new desk	*enough room for the WP*
extra shelving & storage	*for extra files*

Your best interest

But you need to be sure about what aspect is most important to you; If you think hard about it, you might realise that it isn't the money that matters as much as the re-grading to recognise your responsibility and also having a comfortable environment to do the work.

Finding out all you can about your wants gives the clues to how you could plan the bargaining. Your list can give you a wide range of possibilities to plan your strategy.

It's always worth the effort to make light work of any problem. Taking the time to plan what you want from a negotiation always reaps its rewards.

Planning has its value whether you're using the phone, writing a letter, or making a presentation in front of the entire group.

Write down as main headings:

- the facts of what you want to say
- the most important parts and the less important
- the reasons why
- the goals you want to achieve

Then add your supporting evidence to each heading and think about the logical sequence you can make from your facts.

Also think about:

- how many people you're going to be talking to
- how much time you're likely to have

You might also decide the emotional level of how you present the information.

GETTING THE MESSAGE ACROSS

Whether you're talking to someone face to face or speaking to a group, using a phone or writing a letter, it's important that the information you are giving is understood easily.

It's all a question of sorting out what you want to say, and finding a clear way of saying it.

You've done all this work and preparation – it'd be a shame if you spoiled the bargain by not putting your best foot forward in the way you approach it.

It's said that there are four basic ways of behaving and expressing oneself:

self-effacing   always agreeing with another person's point of view, their wishes, their needs. This turns to constant complaints about not getting what you want.

manipulating	putting the other person in a false position by a number of means, including emotional blackmail. Eventually other people believe you are dangerous and will work harder to resist you.
aggressive	determined to get your own way even if it means using threats or force. This is matched by negative force from the other side such as blank refusal, stone-walling, or obstruction.
	All three foregoing ways end with a form of stress; people end up doing something against their will, feeling insecure, feeling a lack of self-respect.
assertive	This is a simpler way forward. It means being clear, direct and unemotional about your needs.

It means making clear statements:

'I want', not *'Would you mind if I asked...'*

Putting your point of view openly and calmly:

'I disagree with your position on this'

'I feel uncomfortable with the way this discussion is developing'

'I don t have the time to do this extra work'

Being assertive

Assertive people feel comfortable with themselves and what they need to say or do. That means they also react well to other people because they're not in competition with them. They can acknowledge them for what and who they are.

Being assertive means you can listen calmly to another person's views without feeling threatened. You can even keep your cool when the other party has quite clearly lost theirs.

Assertive people also use open and relaxed body language. They don't give out threatening signals. They look a person in the eye. They use open gestures. They don't have ruses to distract themselves from the current situation.

Assertiveness is something that can be easily practised on one's own, starting with quite simple situations and working up gradually to the more difficult ones.

First, make your own list of situations in which you feel uncomfortable.

for example •   returning unsatisfactory goods to a shop
   •   complaining to the management about poor service
   •   asking a colleague to take on a chore for you
   •   saying no to a friend who always cadges off you
   •   expressing feelings like fear or dislike
   •   going for an interview
   •   meeting a group of strangers

Spend a little time working out exactly what happens in each situation and how you think you react in each case. Sort them out into an order of difficulty.

Starting with the easiest and most simple situation, you can now plan your own practice to improve on the parts you feel let you down. Work on each separate element until you feel comfortable. Then move on to the next until you feel confident in dealing with the whole situation.

When returning goods you might find yourself:

for example •   feeling hesitant about going into the shop
   •   unable to express what you want clearly
   •   flustered by a response you weren't expecting
   •   worried that they'll say it's your fault

You can practise dealing with all of that, working out what you want from the shop beforehand, rehearsing what you're going to say out loud, thinking ahead for answers to all they might say.

Strategies

This is the serious business of Negotiation. Both sides come to a discussion with points of view and needs which they don't want to lose. Both sides also have goals which they want to win.

Getting there and achieving your targets successfully depend a great deal on how cleverly you can manage and direct the way your negotiation develops.

It becomes a game of knowing when and how to push the discussion forward or hold back, keeping quiet on facts the other side wants to know, giving way, holding tight, balancing concessions and keeping on top of the techniques being used by the other side.

Planning, preparation and practice of what you're going to say at the negotiation gets you well on the way to achieving your targets once you're round the table with the other side.

This chapter takes you through the steps, and ends with further episodes in the Lifescenes to show how the negotiations are working out.

It will include:

preparing a strategy

practising your responses
building self-confidence
some bargaining ploys
confirming the rule book
summarising decisions

dirty tricks

lies and deceptions
below the belt

PREPARING A STRATEGY

So far, it's all been preparation: getting the facts together, working out what you want, finding out what they might want, setting targets, minimum levels and alternatives.

Now you need to organise everything you've learnt to make it all work for you effectively. Every scrap of information you have is worth something in the bargaining process, so it's important to know exactly how you could use it, when to bring it in and how much importance you're going to give it.

Preparation

Organise your information and facts into distinct groups such as:

- your side of the discussion
- their side of the discussion
- common ground
- expert information

Now organise each group into relevant sub-sections - you need to have each special point you want to make supported by facts, expert opinion, examples already agreed, so that you can put your argument across with strength.

Building

1 It's important too, that you really get to know all this information backwards.

Write it out, putting down each point and its supporting information on a separate sheet.

2 Work at it so that you know it from every angle you can think of - which is a very different process from memorising it all parrot-fashion. You need to be able to call on your information at any point of the discussion, so you need it at your fingertips.

3 Work out how you could use what you know. You don't want to put all your cards on the table all at once so you need to plan your moves. You need to:

- start off your side of play
- move it forward if it's stuck
- reinforce your main points
- counteract heavy moves from the other side
- produce 'secret weapons' when you think the other side is getting too much of an advantage.

PRACTISING

However, a negotiation never follows in logical steps. The other side is hardly ever going to have anything like your point of view, your method of thinking, your reasoning.

Learning how to make the discussions work only comes with trial and error - and it's best to practise before you are face to face with the other party.

It's now a question of planning strategies. Your **starting point** is obviously your ideal way for the negotiation to progress:

- you put your case with supporting facts
- the other side responds and puts their case
- both sides agree on the common ground
- both sides discuss the points of difference to see whether they really are differences
- each side compromises, trades and exchanges points until they reach mutual satisfaction

But what if they don't?

A strong strategy will develop, through testing each part of your case against all kinds of possible replies and testing how you yourself can deal with them.

At each point of your argument ask yourself *'what if'*
they...

say 'no'?

have contradictory arguments?

bring in evidence I hadn't thought of?

have different views of the facts?

Try to think of several possible responses to each of your
bargaining points - the main ones and the supporting
ones. Try and work out how you should react effectively to
keep the discussion working for your benefit.

Work hardest at the kind of response that you are really
worried might happen - the more we face up to the worst
possible consequence, the less frightening it becomes.

From all the information you have gathered about the
other side, you should have a very good idea of how they
are likely to respond to you. Try to play the scene in your
imagination. Better still, get a friend to act out the situation
with you and you can work on what happens in it together
- your friend should help you sort out and practise any
particular problems you feel unhappy with.

FEELING GOOD - BUILDING SELF-CONFIDENCE

Most people waste a large amount of energy worrying
about things they don't actually know will happen. They
worry about what the boss might say and do from a
position higher up the system; about what strangers might
be like before they meet them; about losing out on a deal.

It's much more useful to put that energy into working out
exactly what you do know, how you're going to put it
across and how you're going to make the best impression
from the start.

In a negotiation, the way you present your case - the
confidence you give out - is a large part of your
bargaining power. It's very important to let the other side

know from the start that you feel good about your side of the argument.

If you look around you at the people you know, in shops or at work you can easily see where a person with self confidence scores.

Look out for people who:

- smile
- stand up straight
- hold themselves well
- look people in the eye
- show they are interested in other people
- speak calmly and clearly
- take a pride in their dress

ACTING THE PART

Can you tell whether they are doing what comes naturally, or acting a part? Sometimes self-confidence is an act. You may not feel well, you haven't done enough preparation, you feel your case isn't really strong enough. Then you need to work at getting back on a firm foundation. You can become self-confident by the practice of simple techniques and it soon becomes a habit.

It's possible to see instant results from each action on that list: spend a day concentrating on one single part of it at a time and see what happens. For example, many people find that smiling at people stops them feeling on the defensive - they become much more open. If you practise holding yourself well, you start feeling taller, more energetic and more alert.

After all, there's no one else in charge of the signals you give out about yourself - it's up to you to let people know what kind of a person you would like them to think you are! Then you could be half way to winning through.

Rehearsals count

The ideal way to negotiate is to be as cool as you can about the people involved and the situation so that you can concentrate on getting to a satisfactory result, on getting as near as you can to what you want.

Often, you may be discussing a subject that is very important to you and you may have to work quite hard to distance yourself from your emotional involvement. That often means you have to act very differently from what you feel.

But in all negotiation, your first audience ought to be your mirror at home - at least it's neutral and doesn't answer back. It gives you the chance to watch yourself, to practise and to change your presentation just as people try out new hairstyles and make-up and check out the latest fashions for social occasions.

Some people in public life use a mirror to check their performance; it's well known that men use their shaving time to practise speeches and to polish their public face. Many company directors are taught charm and presentation after seeing a video of their unconscious habits. Actors certainly try out new characters in private before taking them to rehearsal for comment from the director.

Your 'playscript' is the negotiating situation. You are going to rehearse your own part in all the situations and responses that you've thought might happen in the course of the discussions:

- presenting your point of view
- counteracting
- standing firm on a fact
- arguing the logic of your own opinion
- trading off minor points
- going for the bigger agreements

Look out for any give-away signs that might tell the other side that you are uncomfortable, under pressure, losing your cool, getting close to the really important part of your case.

Practise the same 'script' with a friend who can throw in arguments and different points when you are not expecting them.

Practise also the arguments and responses in other bargaining situations which you may come across so you can strengthen your techniques to deal with strangers.

SOME BARGAINING PLOYS

Jockeying for position

It's only natural to want to feel that,you have the leading edge on the discussion or that you don t want to be pressurised into agreement. Don't let the other side do all the talking.

Playing for time

If you are put in a spot, it's useful to have some phrases to fall back on to give you more time, like:

"I'll have to look up the figures for that"

"Mr X is our expert on that point, I'll check with him after the meeting."

"Of course this puts quite a new light on the matter. I can't possibly give you an answer today, as we agreed."

"Are you sure you've got it right? I'd be grateful if you would go over the report again in case something has been missed."

Discussion techniques

Opening out the discussion can often be to your advantage. A junior member of the other team may be flattered to be asked for their opinion, and give more away than they should.

Bargaining minor points

It's sometimes to your advantage to spend a long time going over fairly minor points on an agenda in the hope that there will not be time to consider a major one. If you are on a committee with members pushed for time, an important decision can often be made at the end quite quickly.

Questions

Use these to find out more about the other side's intentions. A direct question is often helpful, such as:

"Do you propose to come to a decision today?"

"I'd like a candid view of where you think the hold-ups will be."

Turn the tables

Put the onus on them for commenting on your offer. Don't give away your position at the start, but only talk in response to questions from them.

Half close

This is really one of the most important strategies in negotiation. Aim at reaching agreement on each point as you discuss it. Build on these agreements, so that you have a solid amount of common ground. Then at the end, so much has already been covered that the final clinch could turn out to be a hug.

SEE ➔ p130

DIRTY TRICKS

Unfortunately, many negotiators turn to dirty tricks to try to get the edge over the other side. They are more concerned at winning at all costs and it's very important to recognise the type as soon as you can in your discussions.

Dirty tricks can start from the moment you walk in the door and the first detail to check is the physical position you're offered in the room.

Light A very common trick is to put people with lights or the sun shining straight into their eyes. You are dazzled by the light and it's difficult to read the important visual signals you can get from the other side's faces. You should ask to move your place or to have the blinds drawn.

Seating If you're given lower seats than the other side, you will feel at a disadvantage when talking up to them. If they put you on very much higher seats you can feel ridiculous. When you sit down, make sure that you will be negotiating at the same level as the other side.

Crowds Bargaining with a big organisation often means that you will be dealing with several people on their team. Ask to be told exactly who is going to be at the meeting before you get there so that you have a chance to prepare yourself properly.

Distractions Negotiating one-to-one has other hazards especially if the meeting is in the other party's office. They have all the advantages because it's their territory and they are in charge of the conditions in which you're working.

Watch out for:

- interruptions from the telephone - ask directly if calls can be diverted whilst you are in discussion.
- shuffling papers - ask directly if they would like a pause to sort out the information they seem to be looking for.
- interruptions from colleagues - ask if there is a private conference or interview room where you will not be disturbed.

And there are a lot more underhand methods used in an attempt to deceive, disrupt and sabotage negotiations. But how would you deal with a situation when you are quite sure that the other side is playing dirty? One way, perhaps, is to let them know that **you** are aware of what's happening but at the same time allowing them a bridge so that they can retreat with their self-esteem intact. Jubilantly calling the other side's bluff may prove how clever you are and win you points but you are less likely to be given an easy ride by the opposition in trying to reach a final settlement. Remember, never lose sight of your main objectives.

How else would you deal with a situation if you knew the other side was playing dirty? What 'bridges' can you offer?

THE GARDEN PATH

Very often you'll find that the person with whom you have been negotiating for a considerable time has not actually got the authority to close the final agreement. You get so far down the line and they then tell you that they will now refer the case upwards to someone else. You will have to start the whole process all over again.

This is a very useful delaying tactic when the other side does not want to come to any agreement - the bigger the organisation, the easier it is to sidestep any commitment by referral to a higher authority.

Always find out how much authority has been given to the person with whom you're dealing and be absolutely straight about it. You can ask direct and clear questions like:

'I see my problem here is to do with re-assessing my job description and also the pay I get for the work. Is this a change that you can authorise if you agree my points - or should we just clarify the basic details in question before I take my problem to the personnel department?'

'I am unhappy over discussing this situation without your wife being here. Are you sure that she is going to accept any agreements made by just the two of us?'

'Are you able to finalise details on the size of loan I'm looking for or will you have to refer it to a senior manager?'

LIES AND DECEPTIONS

This is where your homework comes in to tell you that something doesn't ring true about what's being said, what's being offered - and of course about what **isn't** being said.

Use your skills of observation too, a lie often comes with signs of agitation, shifty looks, heightened skin colour.

Challenge anything you find difficult to believe with very straightforward and simple questions:

'What is your evidence for that statement?'

'Please explain how you reach that conclusion?'

'Can you give me more precise information?'

MOVING THE GOAL-POSTS

Just when you think you're getting to an agreeable conclusion, the other side throws in something extra. They might say

"But of course, now we seem to have reached some common ground, I'm sure you can appreciate that before we can actually formalise the agreement we also need to consider....."

And you find yourself facing a set of proposals or demands which you know are going to be impossible to accept.

Other tricks along the same kind of lines are:

changing the purpose of the negotiations in mid-discussion

For example, you may have gone in to discuss your pay-rise and your manager insists on agreeing on a code of behaviour first.

Or, you are trying to agree a share of the housework with your husband and he tries to sidestep by arguing about how you can measure an equal contribution of the chores.

changing the direction of negotiations between sessions

It's quite common to find you leave your first meeting at a certain point which is completely ignored at the start of the next. It feels as though you're starting from the beginning all over again.

putting on the pressure

You feel that the other side is trying to rush through all the points you want acknowledged and are brushing some aside as not important in the time available.

delaying tactics

The opposite to pressure. The other side feels it's in your interest to come to an agreement within a certain time limit. They find any excuse to postpone it – they plead sickness, pressure of work, the difficulties in getting their team together.

BELOW THE BELT

Making personal remarks is one of the most unpleasant forms of attack and it happens to us every day and in every kind of situation - sometimes in formal negotiations where you are representing others. It's not easy to deal with such remarks without jeopardising the talks. The best advice is to keep moving towards your main objectives and behave yourself in an calm, unemotional way.

Antidotes

1 It's important to distance yourself from the harasser - even if you are sitting across the table from them. Take a moment or two to remind yourself that they might be experiencing certain feelings of inadequacy and these feelings are a giveaway which could tell you something to your advantage.

What is the nature of the remark? What does it tell you about the person who makes it? Does it show:

fear of a different culture?

resistance to having a tight-knit group 'invaded'?

testing of status before a so-called 'inferior'?

inadequate personality traits – height, education, vocabulary, strength, qualifications?

transference of a power imbalance elsewhere? Some of the most insistent bottom pinchers are the subordinate partner in the family home.

Here are some giveaways.

"What you women need is a man to look after you" - *is that to hide the fact that he can't get it together to boil an egg?*

"Of course, you people from the third world" - *what kind of an education has he got? He seems to be worried by my B.Tec.*

"You'll find things have got much faster since you started work all those years ago"- *obviously she can't keep up with word-processing herself!*

2 Practise some neutralising replies - you should never show the remarks upset you and you should avoid replying in like manner. That scores a point for your harasser. Luckily, most forms of abuse are fairly limited and can be dealt with by stock replies which you can practise until you feel comfortable with them.

But, whatever kind of harassment it is, it's important to make a point of your reply. Don't rush in at once with any old comment. Make sure you respond with dignity.

Pause (try counting a slow three – five is even more effective).

Look them directly in the eye.

Make a direct statement and make sure it has been heard clearly. Don't get into arguments.

3   Unfortunately, making people stop harassing others is quite difficult. It has become a habit and a defence which is deeply ingrained. However, the law is against it so, if the situation persists, you should take official steps to stop the harasser.

You need to plan this carefully whether it happens to you in a public, or in a private, negotiation. Just as the harasser enjoys abusing your individual liberty, so they will enjoy ganging up with others to refute your story if you make a public complaint.

- Try to find out whether your colleagues have experienced anything similar from your assailant. Try to persuade them to get together with you to make a stronger case. Two, three or four different examples of bad behaviour add to more than a passing joke or a 'little bit of fun'.

- Try to get as many of your other colleagues to understand your experience and to back you up.

- Start by confronting your harasser in public, with a few colleagues around you. Point out formally that his or her behaviour has been noted by several people and that if it doesn't stop you will report them to the union and the management.

- And report them if they don't. Managements are often unaware of what is happening within their company. No management wants to be taken to court for failing to endorse the Equal Opportunities Act.

In a private situation, you should formally confront the harasser. Tell him straight out:

you consider the remarks he makes offensive

you are asking him to stop making them

you want him to concentrate on the specific topics on the agenda of the negotiation

that if he doesn't stop you must ask formally for an observer to be present whilst you continue or you will stop the discussion and go straight to make an official complaint about how the negotiation is being handled.

Too often, we don't make a fuss especially if the harasser is in a position of power over us – an office supervisor, the landlady, garage mechanic, a policeman. If we let them get away with it, it only pushes the problem on to the next person they meet.

A clear, straight unemotional confrontation is the best way to stop such unpleasant games.

ALWAYS CONFIRM THE RULE BOOK

You may feel that it's stuffy, boring and pedantic, but the only way to stop the goal posts moving is to make rules about the negotiations before you start. Quite often, you hear on the news that a team of professional negotiators are spending months just working out the agenda of some major discussions.

This is where that time spent planning and preparing your case brings its rewards. You know exactly what you want to achieve and why. You should also know a good deal about the tactics the other side might play. It's up to you to make sure that you draw up a very clear, direct agenda which won't let in any sudden extra items to unbalance your case.

BEFORE NEGOTIATIONS START

Make your agenda clear

State your aims very clearly and make sure the other side understands and takes note.

Make sure you get the other side to state their aims clearly and completely.

Draw up a list of all the points each side wants to discuss and write them down as the official agenda.

NOTE   Sometimes further points arise as a proper result of the discussions. These are not the same as unexpected extras thrown in to unbalance you and you may want to agree to include them in your fixed agenda.

AGREE A TIMETABLE

Set out targets to be achieved at each meeting and set yourself a time limit for each point you want to discuss. People can waste hours of time waffling on at meetings and a negotiation is no different, but it's quite easy to cut through and bring the conversation back to the proper subject.

There are various useful phrases which bring people back to the point without sounding rude:

"I think we've strayed rather far from the point"

"I'm sure your point is very valid, but it doesn't really affect the matter in discussion"

"Time is running on, could we please get back to the subject?"

If your negotiation is going to carry on over more than one session it's essential to set out an agenda and time-table for **each** session before you start. A break in the middle of negotiations can be quite valuable if used properly. You can consult with advisors or get further information from the group you represent. It gives you time to think and sort out your next steps more clearly.

However, the other side may take it as an excuse to bring several new people on their team. They may also conveniently forget the progress you've achieved at your last meeting.

Make sure you agree:

- the dates of all the sessions in advance
- the agenda to be achieved at the end of each stage
- personnel who will take part at each stage

AT THE END OF EACH MEETING

Make sure that you summarise - out loud, to everyone at the meeting - all the points that you have agreed during the course of the discussions. It is very important that everyone agrees over what has been achieved. It's important also to write them down to remind yourself at the next meeting or, if there are minutes being taken, make sure your summary is reported in full.

Your first task at the start of the next meeting, is to remind everyone of what was agreed last time.

You need to be particular about the formalities in a negotiating situation - even if you are negotiating among friends or with your family. It helps to take some of the steam out of the situation and keep things cool.

Who would like the last biscuit?

1c Buying a car

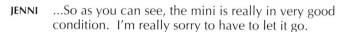

JENNI ...So as you can see, the mini is really in very good condition. I'm really sorry to have to let it go.

ANGELA It certainly goes well. *(looks along the side)* It looks as if there's been some repairs along the side though. Have you been in an accident?

JENNI Oh, nothing serious. My sister had a little scrape in it last year in Birmingham.

ANGELA Your sister? I thought you were the only driver.

JENNI Well we shared the car for a time. And talking about time, goodness it's nearly 5.30. A young couple are coming to see it you know. Of course, I don't want to rush you, and I'd really rather it went to a good home. Shall we say £1,200 for a quick sale, to take account of the scrape?

ANGELA I would rather get a professional opinion I'd like the AA to check it over before I make up my mind.

JENNI Why not save yourself the fee? I tell you what, I'll come down to £1,000. But that has to be my last offer.

ANGELA I'm sorry, but I've worked hard to buy a car. I can't take the risk.

JENNI I see, so you don't trust my word. People like you always have a chip on your shoulder. I don't need to sell it to you. I've had plenty of offers.

ANGELA *(calmly)* I don't think you need to be offensive. I have plenty of cars to see, and I'm sure I will find one that suits me. Thank you for your time.

(later)

GARY You see, what did I tell you? It would have been a rip off. Now Paul's Cortina...

ANGELA Gary! Forget it! Now how about you looking through the ads in the local paper while I check the weekly mags. And don't forget to compare the prices with the 2nd hand car book. And then I'll make us a really good curry. OK?

GARY Angela, you're great!

2c Dispute with neighbours

GREG   I don't know if I can live next door to that woman much longer. I'll give her a real blast. *(Turns hi-fi up. Banging on wall.)*

JANE   I know, but I suppose they are elderly and we do have to live next to them. There must be some way to break through this situation. I wish I knew what it was.

GREG   Well, your mother's the same generation, and she doesn't act like that.

JANE   She's just nicer. Anyway, what would she do? I suppose she'd be round there with a pot of jam.

GARY   That's an idea. What about some apples from our tree? That might sweeten her up. Be a kind of peace offering.

JANE   And why don't you offer to take some of the old man's rubbish to the dump for him? There's a pile outside.

GARY   Well I am going tomorrow. OK, let's give it a whirl.

(later)

MOLLIE   I just thought you might like to taste some of my black-berry and apple Jam, dear. It's a recipe I had from my old Granny. It was kind of Greg to take Dan's rubbish. He's not as strong as he was.

JANE   Greg is kind really. But he just expects everyone to like the same things as he does.

MOLLIE   And I'm afraid I do have a hot Scots temper. You must think us old fusspots. But since my fall, I do have terrible migraines and somehow that thumping music seems to come right through the walls.

JANE   Perhaps I can get Greg to listen on headphones some-times. In fact I might get him a really good pair for his birthday.

3c Complaints at a shop

MARTIN   I'd like to see the manager, please.

TED   I'm afraid he's busy. Can I help you?

MARTIN   No, I need to speak to the manager myself.

TED   Aren't you the guy who came back with that stereo? I've already told you, you have to get on to the manufacturers. It's not our responsibility.

MARTIN   I'm not prepared to discuss it with you. I want to see the manager, please.

TED   OK, Keep cool. I'll see if he's free. *(off)* I'm sorry, Mr Jones. That guy just won't leave. He insists on seeing you.

MR JONES   Oh, very well. *(to Martin)* Now young man, what is it?

MARTIN   I think you know what the problem is. This stereo I bought last Saturday has drop-out on the right channel and I want a replacement.

MR JONES   My assistant has already explained to you....

MARTIN   Your assistant doesn't know his facts. I've checked with the Consumers' Advice Bureau and they tell me you have an obligation to change faulty goods within a reasonable time after purchase. And I came back on Monday morning having bought the stereo on Saturday. That must be reasonable enough.

MR JONES   I'm sorry, young man, I'm afraid we have none of that model in stock.

MARTIN   In that case, I'll take a different one. I should like to see the model in the window priced £97.99, please.

MR JONES   It's not our usual practice. But since you insist... Ted, would you show the young gentleman the new TG 1015?

4c   Seeing the bank manager

MRS ROBERTSON	Thank you for sending me your revised business plan in advance. I've gone through it carefully and it seems well thought out. But I would like to go through some of the figures in the cash flow. As you must realise, at the end of the day, it's the top line, not the bottom line that counts. So could you tell me how definite these orders are, or are they just estimates?
JO	I've had firm orders which would cover all the sales figures up to next July. That's when there may be a break during holiday time. The receipts will cover all my running costs, but I need to put in some modern kitchen equipment. And as you know, marketing is all-important, so I also have to start a marketing drive in January. I'm getting in a specialist marketing company. That's why I'm asking for an overdraft facility.
MRS ROBERTSON	Let's take the two items separately. What do you think the marketing drive would cost?
JO	I'm thinking of a budget of around £3,000.
MRS ROBERTSON	Well, I'm prepared to extend your overdraft to cover that figure, until the end of July.
JO	Good. That should give me time to drum up some customers.
MRS ROBERTSON	Then we're agreed. But I believe the bank would prefer to make you a loan for capital expenditure. I assume £2,000 would be the sum required?
JO	Yes that's right. It's in the cash flow. Well, I could cover the loan if I started repayments in the new year, when my customers start their payments to me.
MRS ROBERTSON	I think that would be in order. Right, I'll get the agreement drawn up, including our first call on your securities. Good luck with the business!
JO	Thank you. You've been very helpful.

5c Changes at work

TONY I've had a word with the Board, as I promised. But I'm afraid that they don't want to go along with overtime at the week-end for shift workers. The Director of Personnel said it would create difficulties with the Union over conditions of work, and the Financial Director said all that had been looked into and it was not cost-effective.

JAMES But you agreed with me...

TONY Of course I sympathise, but it's not my decision. I'm afraid. Now, as far as the productivity goes, the Board have asked me to bring in a time-and-motion study team.

JAMES This is disgraceful! If the company is treating us in this manner, I don't think the team will find my operators prepared to be very helpful.

TONY Are you threatening me? That's not very wise in your position, James.

JAMES How do you mean, in my position?

TONY You may find that the time-and-motion team will suggest bringing in trained supervisors from outside.

JAMES I see. Then it seems I have no option but to pass on the Board's decision to my workers.

TONY I knew you'd see it our way, old chap.

6c Dealing with harassment

DAVE	*(joining the women in the canteen)* Hallo girls! Having a tea break then? Hey Bob, these two can never keep up with the men! Tell you what, I'll give you a hand if you give us a cuddle. I've always fancied a threesome.
LOU	*(ignoring him)* Gina, Look who's just walked in! I'm surprised his wife let him out in that filthy sweater.
GINA	Give over. Dave wouldn't have a wife. Can you imagine anyone living with that creep?
LOU	Now you mention it, no I can't. If he treated his wife like he does us, she'd have walked out years ago.
DAVE	Are you talking about me, darling?
GINA	Goodness, it speaks! Lou, did you hear that?
LOU	Well, it's got a big mouth, hasn't it?
DAVE	Now look here, what's going on?
LOU	*(taking a deep breath)* Dave, Gina and I have had enough of your big mouth, putting us down the whole time. We work here, and we do a good job. If you are really so threatened by two women, then I suggest you take your talents somewhere else where they'll be appreciated. Because they're not appreciated by us.
DAVE	Oh come on. Can't you take a joke?
GINA	Dave, earning your living in this day and age is not a joke, it's deadly serious. Or hadn't you noticed? As far as Louise and I are concerned, we are employed by this firm and we are good workers. If you continue your harassment, we intend to go straight to the boss. And if we don't get satisfaction, then we'll go to the courts. I'm quite prepared to go as far as it takes.
LOU	And so am I.
GINA	So you'd better decide Dave. Which is it going to be? Are you going to accept us as workers on an equal basis with the others, or do we have to go the boss? The choice is yours.

7c Changes at the office

MRS CAPLIN	I've given a lot of thought to what you said last time we met, and I think I've come up with a solution. Before we begin, I take it if we can solve the problem. You do both feel happy handling work in this department and would like to stay.
JOHN	Yes. It's a good team, and there's enough of a challenge.
IRENE	I'm not sure. I meant what I said about consultation.
MRS CAPLIN	All right. Well this is what I propose. As you both know, Nelson in design has worked one before. If you agree to join him, he is prepared to lead you both as a team for a few months to handle all our typesetting. You will of course receive an intensive training course from the suppliers, but Nelson will be responsible for all the final checking, and will take on some of the work.
	I also suggest that we four meet regularly, at least once a week to start with, to check on any problems, and iron them out as they occur. This will include monitoring your work loads, and also your time in front of the screen. How does that seem?
IRENE	I'd like to think it over. My first reaction is it seems fair. But I don't want to get stuck in keyboard work.
JOHN	Yes, that goes for me too.
MRS CAPLIN	Then I have one further proposal. At the end of, say, six months, the firm will offer you a training attachment to another section. Irene, you might like to consider design and John, it could be editorial for you. Why don't we all meet tomorrow and hammer out a decision. I'll ask Nelson to come along too.

8c An interview with the boss

GUY   Well, how was your meeting?

MARK   Oh I reckon Judy's all right when you know how to handle her.

GUY   Great! Here's a guy who was scared to see the boss yesterday, and today she's eating out of his hand. What did you feed her, boy, monkey nuts?

MARK   Well, if you must know, I followed your advice, big brother. I wrote my points down on a card and took her through them carefully. And she listened.

GUY   People do if they know what the hell you are on about. And I take it we were wearing that new tweed jacket and the clean shirt we're wearing today? That muted blue suits you.

MARK   Thanks a lot! Actually, you were right. Looking good gave me a lot more confidence to explain what I was after.

GUY   And knowing how to say it clinched the interview. Great! Your turn to buy me a beer.

9c Union negotiations

HARRY I don't have good news to report, lads. After our special meeting last week I sent young Renfrew a detailed outline of our proposals and we had a long meeting this morning. He won't budge.

PAT I could have told you you were wasting your breath. That boy has no feeling for the business. His father would turn in his grave.

HARRY Well, he showed me the books. It's clear enough he has to cut costs to keep output going. It's just that our skills don't meet the requirements of the company as he sees it for the future.

PAT And I suppose that knowledge is going to pay our wages!

HARRY No. But I've been doing some homework too. This is a port with a tradition of boatbuilding, right?

ALI Right. And there are still firms that believe in the old crafts.

HARRY So, I believe we could sell our labour as a craft team. I reckon we could earn a decent living as a boatbuilding cooperative. We've master skills in lofting, shaping, fitting and finishing. If Renfrews get rid of us, we'll be entitled to decent compensation. If we use that compensation as capital to set ourselves up in our own workshop we could offer our services to all the businesses in our area.

ALI My nephew doesn't like GRP work. He might join us. We'd need some youngsters.

HARRY And my Susan looked interested last night when I was telling her and Dora about the boss. No, Pat. I'm not having you say no. If a girl's as good as a lad, and she is, she should have the same chance. That's how it's always been in my family.

We'll have to cost it right from the bottom. I can't afford to lose.

Neither can any of us. We have to move very carefully. It will mean looking out for a suitable yard. Susan has agreed to sit down with me to do initial costings and make a draft business plan to submit to the bank. Bob, with your contacts, would you be willing to make an informal approach to local yards? Pat, you're the best craftsman of us all, so you're the best person to draw up a promotion document of what we can offer our clients. Now, shall we meet the same time next week? I should have some idea of the compensation payments from Renfrews by then.

10c A public campaign

ANNE	Good afternoon, I'm Anne Jennings, and these are my colleagues John Patterson and Marie Kopolski from the City Centre Campaign. Before we begin, I'd just like to mention that we represent a number of interests in the town who are all anxious that the Council does not rush into a decision about the town centre without considering all the factors.
COUNCILLOR MILLAR	We're always very pleased to hear the views of our ratepayers. But, Mrs Jennings, I am sure I don't need to remind your group why the Council wishes to proceed with this development. Frankly, it's a question of making the best use of our resources, and the hotel group has made us a very good offer.
ANNE	Yes, but their scheme involves pulling down buildings, which we believe could be put to use in a different way. John Patterson has been looking into alternatives and his committee have also drawn up outline costings. John, would you explain?
JOHN	Well, as I see it, the Council needs to sell some of the property to release funds for capital expenditure, and also to obtain income from leasing. We believe that

both objectives could be achieved by restoring or refurbishing the existing buildings so that some could be sold after restoration, and some could be rented out to local and incoming small businesses. For instance, hi-tech firms now realise that the solid walls and high ceilings of old warehouses may be very appropriate for their purposes, providing that suitable air-cleaning and ventilation systems can be installed. I have here a list of the buildings that could be adapted for such use, with approximate costs for refurbishment and their future sale value.

MARIE And I have been in touch with a number of small businesses in the area who have expressed interest in short-term rentals.

COUNCILLOR MILLAR *(looking through)* Yes, this seems to be very impressive. But of course you do realise that our other important aim is to bring more employment into the town?

JOHN That is why we've also included a hotel complex based round the old Central Hotel, but with the addition of a modern conference annexe on the south side, away from the road. This would make use of the old timber yard land. Of course the designs would need to be in keeping with the present buildings.

ANNE Obviously our group doesn't want to stand in the way of development, but we are anxious to maximise the potential for all sides, not least to ourselves as ratepayers!

COUNCILLOR MILLAR I agree that we may have some aims in common and perhaps we may be able to accommodate some of your ideas. Very well, I am prepared to discuss your plans at the Planning Committee next week. Perhaps you would be available to answer questions if necessary?

11c   Pitching for new work

SAHIR   We've come to see you, Mr McPherson, because we believe that a firm like ours would be able to provide you with a dedicated service in both your systems management and your public relations.

MCPHERSON   You're a fairly new company, I believe?

SAHIR   Yes, that's true. All our directors have come from large companies, so we know the latest thinking on corporate planning. In essence, we could offer you large firm experience with small firm overheads.

JAMILLA   We have already carried out systems management for four firms in the area. They would, I know, be happy to give us a reference.

MCPHERSON   What else would you be able to offer JBM if we were to take you on?

JAMILLA   As a small local firm, we are able to respond quickly to changing situations. One of our strengths is our flexibility.

MCPHERSON   Systems management is very different from the problems of corporate affairs. What makes you think you could combine the two?

SAHIR   Two of our directors moved from a public relations firm in London - they came for personal reasons - but they have wide contacts in the media and considerable experience with companies in your line of business. One of them was responsible for the 'Cook a Cookie' campaign, which was so successful last year.

MCPHERSON   What do you think is the most important side of Public Relations?

JAMILLA   We believe that large companies should be part of the community. I know that you already have sporting links with the area. We would like to develop a higher profile in others - for instance in expanding the local community arts centre. The costs should not be too great, and since so many of your workers and their families use the centre, it would make you one of the most well-known of the sponsors.

SAHIR We have drawn up an outline proposal of the services we can offer and how we would propose to carry them out. I realise that there would be modifications when we learn more about your work from the inside, but it should provide a framework for further discussions, if you would be willing to study it.

Working together

How to get to the right conclusion by working your way through to agreement.

This chapter brings together all the techniques and skills discussed in the rest of the book to channel them into the process of negotiation.

- first steps
- who starts?
- your turn
- testing
- carrots
- the ancient art
- half-closes
- problems
- closing the deal

FIRST STEPS

It doesn't matter whether you're about to meet a senior executive of your company or to settle an argument with your family. You need to make sure you are in the right frame of mind:

- cool
- clear-thinking
- alert
- and in control of yourself

You want to feel that you can avoid any kind of emotional upset, that you are calmly focussing on the matter in hand and its successful outcome.

You are not going to be diverted by anyone or anything else.

You need to be on your toes and mentally flexible. In a negotiation, you constantly adjust your thinking as the game crosses backwards and forwards between the parties involved.

It's important to concentrate your full attention on the game.

Take a few deep breaths to collect yourself before you go in to meet the other side face to face.

WHO STARTS?

Always try to get the other side to make the opening move. It doesn't matter if you're the one who has actually asked for the meeting to happen and therefore might feel that the other side is waiting for you to open.

It's in your interest to find where the other side has chosen to start from. This is particularly important in a business situation. You need to try to judge how far away they are from the goals you want to reach.

If their starting point is quite close, you may find there are only a few points to discuss and agree before you can come to a conclusion.

If they are starting a long way away from you, you'll need to find out as quickly as you can whether that's just an opening try-on and they will then move from it quite fast, or whether you are going to have to draw on your reserve arguments to pull them towards you bit by bit.

Getting them to start first may tell you their frame of mind. Are they ...

sympathetic to your case?

hostile?

muddled?

prepared?

playing hard?

playing soft?

interested?

not very interested?

antagonistic?

SEE � p94

You can then start to respond to their case in the appropriate manner. It's something you should be quite happy to do if you've prepared for it before the meeting.

YOUR TURN

Make a clear statement about your case.

Keep it simple, sticking to the main points.

Make sure you cover **all** the basic points you want included.

Don't start giving details, arguments, or qualifying statements.

Don't blow your chances by revealing your back-up facts and figures.

Don't qualify your proposal with 'ifs' and 'buts'.

Then Set out your conditions, make a clear statement about what you expect the other side to do too.

Keep it short and simple.

Then keep quiet.

Don't be tempted to rush in and say something if there's an aching silence. You want the other side to respond to what you have said. If you let them off the hook by talking, you may very well lose out on a constructive response. No-one likes being challenged to fill a silence with a serious, valid response that everyone is listening for.

Wait for them to answer, and listen carefully to how they reply and what they say.

TESTING

SEE ➜ p64 Each side is going to make assumptions about what the other has said. This information is received through formal and informal communication.

From what you hear, note:

- straight facts
- the tone of voice
- vocabulary
- style of presentation

It's important to test these out to make sure you've got it right.

SEE ➝ p85 You find out more by asking questions.

Are you talking about the same problem? Make sure you confirm those interests and solutions that you have in common.

Try to find out whether you can modify your response to match the other side's.

Try to find out whether there are any unspoken interests that might be colouring their response.

Try to find out which points are the most and the least important to them - ie what does their hand of cards contain?

CARROTS

By giving out some items of information, you may learn a lot more from how the other side responds.

You want to find out how far you can agree and reach your goal on your original expectation and then how much you will have to change.

Start by opening a discussion on an item of information you've designated as low down on your list of aims and see what it brings back. See if you can also get an agreement on your point.

Try another on a different angle.

This way you can very quickly learn what is interesting and important. You are 'spending minor issues to get back information and to test the attitudes to your major issues.

This is where sorting out your issues and priorities comes into its own.

You can also try out different styles of behaviour at this level to see how you're going to work together.

for example If you're cool, try putting in a little warmth on one point to gauge the effect.

If you're practical and business-like, soften up a bit.

THE ANCIENT ART

Bargaining is a way of life all over the world. You never ever take the first offer as serious and the fun of the technique is the manoeuvring with the other side to get to an agreement.

You can think of it as a game, with classic moves and responses:

offer	*at a price far too high*
counter-offer	*at a price far too low*
impasse	*both sides declare the other offer impossible*

Try to find out what the other's motives are:

- selling at a profit
- buying at the cheapest price
- coming down in price to get a quick sale
- raising the offer because the quality is good

From time to time, there are diversions:

- withdrawing from the process
- losing interest
- pretending that the price is final

From time to time, there are reconciliations:

- talk about the weather
- share confidences about the family
- find mutual interests outside the business

And when this has gone on enough and each side feels that they have got to know and trust the other - that they're not doing a rip-off - it all reaches agreement.

In some places, the bargaining for an important item such as a valuable antique can go on over several weeks.

The same procedures happen in principle in any formal negotiating situation.

HALF-CLOSES

This is a standard sales technique to try to get the other side so committed to various aspects of the proposal throughout the discussions that they cannot really justify refusing to say "yes" finally to the full package.

for example you are negotiating for a pay-rise and new office furniture because your boss thinks you work well enough on your own to be delegated extra tasks.

You want to get agreement:

- that you do indeed have extra work
- that your boss thinks you can do more
- that you do the work on your own initiative
- that your fellow workers do not do this
- but the trouble is the extra paper and filing

Having agreed you do all this extra activity - and all of this is pure fact - they cannot start arguing against the fact you've both agreed when you start on your main points.

Make sure you know your list of half-closes.

You can also **half-close** at each stage of the negotiation by going over the ground you've covered and asking the other side to agree on what has happened so far. It's another short step along the way to your goal. Several small steps make the final agreement much easier.

PROBLEMS

You could find yourself facing an impasse - nobody is prepared to budge an inch from their fixed opening positions.

Don't push, don't try to break the deadlock then and there.

- What is the real cause of this deadlock?
- Are there any options left unexplored?
- Are there any new tactics we can use?
- Is this the time to drop the demands to the lowest acceptable?

It really helps to work out this kind of situation with another person. It's very nice if you are part of a team that can put all its heads together. If you're by yourself, a good way to see through problems is by writing down the options.

Brainstorming Do this again. Look for a free association of ideas roughly connected with the problem. Focus on it and then give yourself five minutes to let possible options flow out of your mind onto that sheet of paper. Don't stop to analyse or criticise what you're writing.

Only start extracting the most promising ideas from the fantasy when you've given yourself that good five minutes.

There are a lot of accepted methods to help people sort out their thoughts:

- free flow association
- linked cells
- tree structure

In most of them the key is writing down the possibilities and then sorting them out.

TAKE YOUR TIME

It always seems quicker and cleaner to get an agreement fast - but beware you don't cut corners.

Take your time in considering the options

You can use a phrase like *"I'd like to take a moment to consider that..."*

Take time to ask further questions when considering the options.

Use time to think positively so you don't agree to something just because you feel you're being hassled.

Use time as a delaying tactic to gain more information about an offer. If you don't answer and look expectant, you may find some more information is suddenly blurted out unguardedly.

Take your time to probe and test the response to as many of your points as you can.

In negotiating you want to make sure that the time you have available is going to get you the best possible conclusion.

CLOSING THE DEAL

It's often quite difficult to start in on the final stretch.

Make sure that you've covered every point that you wanted to discuss and that there's nothing more outstanding.

A good way in is to start by summarising the entire discussion so far, taking great care to emphasise the points already agreed by both sides and the points conceded by each side.

Which now leaves the final item on the agenda.

You start by making a formal offer - rather in the way the whole negotiation began, right at the beginning.

You make a clear statement, covering all your points, and setting out the goal you're now aiming for. This has most likely changed as a result of all the points you've agreed along the way, those 'Half-Closes'.

Then wait for the response.

If you have worked well at each point from your opening statement onwards, this final step should almost be merely a formality.

Then all that's left are the details of sorting out any written agreement or contract, which should include all the points covered.

And the traditional seal on the agreement is to shake hands on it.

Further reading

Accelerated Learning by Colin Rose
(pub. Topaz Publishing)

The Art of Negotiating by Gerard I. Nierenberg
(pub. Pocket Books)

Assertive Woman by Phelps & Austin
(pub. Impact Publishers)

Bargaining for Results by John Winkler (pub. Pan)

Don't Say Yes When You Want to Say No by Herbert
Fensterheim and Jean Baer (pub. Futura)

Everything is Negotiable by Gavin Kennedy (pub. Arrow)

Frogs into Princes by Richard Bandler and John Grinder
(pub. Real People Press)

Getting to Yes by Roger Risher and William Ury
(pub. Arrow)

Influencing with Integrity by Genie Z. Laborde
(pub. Syntony Inc.)

The Negotiating Game by Chester L. Karras
(pub. Collins)

*People Skills: How to Assert Yourself, Listen to Others &
Avoid Conflict* by Robert Bolton (pub. Prentice-Hall)

Take 10 to Grow by Franklin D. Cordell and Gale R.
Gieblek (pub. Argus Communications)

When I Say No I Feel Guilty by Manuel J. Smith
(pub. Bantam Books)

*Women as Winners: Transactional Analysis for Personal
Growth* by Dorothy Jongeward & Andrew Scott
(pub. Addison Wesley)

Written and produced by:
Worsley Wheen Productions
P.O. Box 588
London NW2 6SQ

Designed by Eugenie Dodd

Drawings by Roger Smith

Cover photographs by Sunil Gupta

Research by Clemencia Faulder

Set on Apple Macintosh by Deadline Typesetting

WWP wish to thank the following people and organisations for their advice and help:

Marcel Anciano

Joan Blackham

Gillian Edwards and students from The Actors Institute

Claire Deane, *Gateway Interpersonal Skills Training*

Regan Masters, *UK Centre for Neuro-Linguistic Programming*

Lucy Green

Published by:
The Careers and Occupational Information Centre
Moorfoot
Sheffield S1 4PQ

ISBN 0-86110-484/6

Further copies of this book and information about the wide range of literature and other related material produced by COIC, including details of prices can be obtained by writing to:

COIC Sales, Rm W1101
Moorfoot
Sheffield S1 4PQ

See COIC on Prestel *270#